DATE DUE

FEB 10 2009

Multiple Origins, Uncertain Destinies

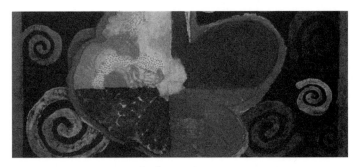

Hispanics and the American Future

Panel on Hispanics in the United States

Marta Tienda and Faith Mitchell, *Editors*

Committee on Population

Division of Behavioral and Social Sciences and Education

NATIONAL RESEARCH COUNCIL
OF THE NATIONAL ACADEMIES

THE NATIONAL ACADEMIES PRESS
Washington, D.C.
www.nap.edu

9888409

THE NATIONAL ACADEMIES PRESS 500 Fifth Street, N.W. Washington, DC 20001

NOTICE: The project that is the subject of this report was approved by the Governing Board of the National Research Council, whose members are drawn from the councils of the National Academy of Sciences, the National Academy of Engineering, and the Institute of Medicine. The members of the committee responsible for the report were chosen for their special competences and with regard for appropriate balance.

This study was supported by Contract No. N01-OD-4-2139, TO #123 between the National Academy of Sciences and the National Institute of Child Health and Human Development, the National Cancer Institute, the Office of Behavioral and Social Sciences Research, the National Institute of Mental Health, and the National Institute on Aging of the National Institutes of Health; the U.S. Census Bureau; the National Center for Health Statistics; the National Institute for Occupational Safety and Health; the Andrew W. Mellon Foundation, the Robert Wood Johnson Foundation, the California HealthCare Foundations, and the California Endowment.

Library of Congress Cataloging-in-Publication Data

Multiple origins, uncertain destinies : Hispanics and the American future : panel on Hispanics in the United States / Marta Tienda and Faith Mitchell, editors.
   p. cm.
   "Committee on Population, Division of Behavioral and Social Sciences and Education."
   Includes bibliographical references and index.
   ISBN 0-309-09667-7 (hardcover book) — ISBN 0-309-55087-4 (pdfs) 1. Hispanic Americans—Social conditions—Statistics. 2. Hispanic Americans—Economic conditions—Statistics. 3. Hispanic Americans—Government policy. 4. United States—Ethnic relations—Statistics. 5. United States—Population—Statistics. I. Tienda, Marta. II. Mitchell, Faith. III. National Research Council. Division of Behavioral and Social Sciences and Education.
   E184.S75M85 2006
   305.868'073090511—dc22

                                        2006000204

Additional copies of this report are available from the National Academies Press, 500 Fifth Street, N.W., Lockbox 285, Washington, DC 20055; (800) 624-6242 or (202) 334-3313 (in the Washington metropolitan area); http://www.nap.edu.

Printed in the United States of America.

Cover credit: Juan Sánchez, *Soles y Flores para Liora* (1997). Copyright by the artist; used with permission.

Suggested citation: National Research Council (2006). *Multiple Origins, Uncertain Destinies: Hispanics and the American Future.* Panel on Hispanics in the United States. M. Tienda and F. Mitchell, eds. Committee on Population, Division of Behavioral and Social Sciences and Education. Washington, DC: The National Academies Press.

THE NATIONAL ACADEMIES
Advisers to the Nation on Science, Engineering, and Medicine

The **National Academy of Sciences** is a private, nonprofit, self-perpetuating society of distinguished scholars engaged in scientific and engineering research, dedicated to the furtherance of science and technology and to their use for the general welfare. Upon the authority of the charter granted to it by the Congress in 1863, the Academy has a mandate that requires it to advise the federal government on scientific and technical matters. Dr. Ralph J. Cicerone is president of the National Academy of Sciences.

The **National Academy of Engineering** was established in 1964, under the charter of the National Academy of Sciences, as a parallel organization of outstanding engineers. It is autonomous in its administration and in the selection of its members, sharing with the National Academy of Sciences the responsibility for advising the federal government. The National Academy of Engineering also sponsors engineering programs aimed at meeting national needs, encourages education and research, and recognizes the superior achievements of engineers. Dr. Wm. A. Wulf is president of the National Academy of Engineering.

The **Institute of Medicine** was established in 1970 by the National Academy of Sciences to secure the services of eminent members of appropriate professions in the examination of policy matters pertaining to the health of the public. The Institute acts under the responsibility given to the National Academy of Sciences by its congressional charter to be an adviser to the federal government and, upon its own initiative, to identify issues of medical care, research, and education. Dr. Harvey V. Fineberg is president of the Institute of Medicine.

The **National Research Council** was organized by the National Academy of Sciences in 1916 to associate the broad community of science and technology with the Academy's purposes of furthering knowledge and advising the federal government. Functioning in accordance with general policies determined by the Academy, the Council has become the principal operating agency of both the National Academy of Sciences and the National Academy of Engineering in providing services to the government, the public, and the scientific and engineering communities. The Council is administered jointly by both Academies and the Institute of Medicine. Dr. Ralph J. Cicerone and Dr. Wm. A. Wulf are chair and vice chair, respectively, of the National Research Council.

www.national-academies.org

PANEL ON HISPANICS IN THE UNITED STATES

MARTA TIENDA (*Chair*), Department of Sociology, Woodrow Wilson
School of Public and International Affairs and Office of Population
Research, Princeton University
LOUIS DESIPIO, Department of Political Science and Chicano/Latino
Studies Program, University of California, Irvine
JORGE DURAND, Social Anthropology, University of Guadalajara, Mexico
JOSÉ J. ESCARCE, David Geffen School of Medicine, UCLA and RAND,
California
V. JOSEPH HOTZ, Department of Economics, University of California,
Los Angeles
NANCY S. LANDALE, Department of Sociology, Pennsylvania State
University
CORDELIA W. REIMERS, Department of Economics, Hunter College and
the Graduate School, City University of New York
RUBÉN G. RUMBAUT, Department of Sociology and Center for Research
on Immigration, Population, and Public Policy, University of California,
Irvine
BARBARA SCHNEIDER, Department of Sociology, University of Chicago
EDWARD TELLES, Department of Sociology, University of California,
Los Angeles
STEVEN J. TREJO, Department of Economics, University of Texas at Austin
PETER WARD, Department of Sociology, University of Texas at Austin*

National Research Council Staff

BARNEY COHEN, *Director, Committee on Population*
FAITH MITCHELL, *Senior Program Officer*
ANA-MARIA IGNAT, *Senior Program Assistant***
ANTHONY S. MANN, *Senior Program Assistant*
AMY GAWAD, *Research Associate****

---

*Until January 2004
**Until November 2004
***Until December 2004

COMMITTEE ON POPULATION

Acknowledgments

With the release of the results of the 2000 census, the growing role of Hispanics in the United States became apparent. Hispanics are now the country's largest minority. Cognizant of the important implications this demographic change would have for the United States, staff of the National Research Council (NRC) suggested it was an appropriate time for a study that would capture social and economic dimensions of the current situation and provide a baseline for future research. The proposed project would also build on prior NRC reports on the status of minority Americans, including *America Becoming: Racial Trends and Their Consequences* (2001) and *A Common Destiny: Blacks and American Society* (1989).

As a first step in developing a study, the NRC convened a planning meeting in 2001, chaired by Marta Tienda, to clarify key issues regarding Hispanics in the United States. This was followed in 2002 by a meeting on emerging issues in Hispanic health, chaired by E. Richard Brown, which was sponsored by the Office of Behavioral and Social Sciences Research of the National Institutes of Health. That meeting brought together experts in demography, public health, medicine, sociology, psychiatry, and other fields to examine key issues related to Hispanic health and well-being and resulted in the report *Emerging Issues in Hispanic Health: Summary of a Workshop* (2002).

With support from the National Institute of Child Health and Human Development, the National Cancer Institute, the Office of Behavioral and Social Sciences Research, the National Institute of Mental Health, and the

National Institute on Aging of the National Institutes of Health; the U.S. Census Bureau; the National Center for Health Statistics; the National Institute for Occupational Safety and Health; the Andrew W. Mellon Foundation, the Robert Wood Johnson Foundation, the California HealthCare Foundations, and the California Endowment, a major study of Hispanics was begun. This report is the product of that study by a panel of experts convened by the National Academies. This report has a companion volume, *Hispanics and the Future of America,* which presents the detailed analyses that underlie much of the discussion in this report. We thank first the sponsors of the project. Their recognition of the timeliness of a study on Hispanics made possible what we believe is a far-reaching and provoking look at the nation's fastest-growing minority population.

We thank the following individuals for their workshop presentations and other contributions to this volume: Jorge Del Pinal, Patricia Fernández-Kelly, Claudia Galindo, John Gallegos, Eugene Garcia, Roberto Gonzalez, John Iceland, J. Gerardo Lopez, Maria Lopez-Freeman, Elizabeth Martin, Jeff Morenoff, Chandra Muller, Jeff Passel, Sean Reardon, Catherine Riegle-Crumb, Jerry Valadez, William A. Vega, Bruce Western, and Marilyn Winkleby.

We also thank Jeff Evans and Roberto Suro for their contributions to the panel's thinking and writing, Charles V. Morgan for preparing data for the panel's analysis, Rona Briere for her editorial contributions, and Yasmin Ramirez for her assistance with the artwork. We very much appreciate Carmen Lomas Garza, Freddy Rodriguez, Ixrael Rodriguez, Juan Sánchez, Nitza Tufiño, Julio Valdez, Patssi Valdez, and Kathy Vargas for permissions to reproduce their artwork. Among the NRC staff, special thanks are due to Barney Cohen, intern Nicole Ganzekaufer, Amy Gawad, Eugenia Grohman, Ana-Maria Ignat, Anthony Mann, Jane Ross, Kirsten Sampson Snyder, and Yvonne Wise.

Special thanks are due to the panel members, who not only contributed to the lively and at times intense analysis presented in this volume, but who also authored or coauthored the papers in our companion volume.

This report has been reviewed in draft form by individuals chosen for their diverse perspectives and technical expertise, in accordance with procedures approved by the NRC's Report Review Committee. The purpose of this independent review is to provide candid and critical comments that will assist the institution in making its published report as sound as possible and to ensure that the report meets institutional standards for objectivity, evidence, and responsiveness to the study charge. The review comments and draft manuscript remain confidential to protect the integrity of the deliberative process. We thank the following individuals for their review of this report: Richard D. Alba, Department of Sociology, State University of New York at Albany; Luis A. Diaz, Department of Dermatology, University of North Carolina School of Medicine; Reynolds Farley, Population Studies Center, University of Michigan; Patricia Gándara, School of Education, University of California, Davis; Jennifer L. Hochschild, Government Department, Harvard University; Robert A. Hummer, Population Research Center, University of Texas at Austin; John R. Logan, Spatial Structures in the Social Sciences, Brown University; B. Lindsay Lowell, Institute for the Study of International Migration, Georgetown University; Alba Ortiz, Office of Bilingual Education, University of Texas at Austin; Richard Santos, College of Arts and Sciences, University of New Mexico; Marcelo M. Suárez-Orozco, Immigration Studies, New York University; and Mary C. Waters, Sociology Department, Harvard University.

Although the reviewers listed have provided many constructive comments and suggestions, they were not asked to endorse the conclusions and recommendations nor did they see the final draft of the report before its release. The review of this report was overseen by Charles Hirschman, Department of Sociology, University of Washington, and Ron Lee, Department of Demography, University of California, Berkeley. Appointed by the NRC, they were responsible for making certain that an independent examination of this report was carried out in accordance with institutional procedures and that all review comments were carefully considered. Responsibility for the final content of this report rests entirely with the authoring committee and the institution.

Marta Tienda, *Chair,* and Faith Mitchell, *Study Director*
Panel on Hispanics in the United States

Contents

Executive Summary   3

     Hispanic Identity, 4
     Social Integration and Mobility, 4
     Uncertain Futures, 7

1   Introduction   13

     Notes, 16

2   Multiple Origins, Hispanic Portrait   19

     Hispanic Roots, 20
     A Contemporary Profile, 22
     Legal Status, 27
     Conclusion, 32
     Notes, 33

3   Defining Hispanicity: *E Pluribus Unum* or *E Pluribus Plures?*   37

     Origins of Hispanic Identity, 38
     The Shifting Concept of Race, 40
     Español or English?, 45

Conclusion, 50
Notes, 52

4   The Challenges of Integration   57

The Changing Social Contract, 57
Economic Trends, 58
Coming of Age in an Aging Society, 60
Hispanic Dispersal, 64
    Paradoxes of Place, 65
    Engines of Growth, 66
    Uncertain Promises, 67
Political Voice, 68
Conclusion, 73
Notes, 73

5   Realms of Integration: Family, Education, Work, and Health   77

Family and Living Arrangements, 77
Schools and Education, 80
    Early Beginnings, 82
    Primary and Middle Years, 84
    Secondary School and Beyond, 85
Economic Well-Being, 87
    Employment and Earnings, 88
    Household Income, 93
    Poverty and Wealth Among Hispanics, 96
Health Status and Access to Care, 99
    Health Status and Behaviors, 100
    Access to Quality Care, 103
Conclusion, 106
Notes, 108

6   Uncertain Destinies   115

Diversity, Identity, and Assimilation, 117
    Hispanicity as a Panethnic Identity, 117
    Sociocultural Transformation, 120
    The Costs of Assimilation, 121

Socioeconomic Mobility, 123
An Uncertain Future, 125
Notes, 127

References   129

Appendixes

A   Methods   139

B   Biographical Sketches of Panel Members and Staff   143

C   Contents: *Hispanics and the Future of America*   149

Index   151

Multiple Origins, Uncertain Destinies

Carmen Lomas Garza
Cama Para Sueños (bed for dreams) (1985)
Copyright by the artist; used with permission.

Executive Summary

Currently the nation's largest ethnic minority, Hispanics are one of the fastest-growing segments of the U.S. population, and they will remain so for the foreseeable future. Numbering over 40 million today, Hispanics are growing by more than 1.5 million annually, from both continuing immigration and natural increase. If current demographic trends continue, nearly 1 in 4 U.S. residents will be Hispanic, or of Hispanic ancestry, by 2030—just a generation hence—up from about 1 in 7 in 2000. Until recently, Hispanics were concentrated in the largest cities in Texas and California, as well as Chicago, New York, and Miami. Now they are scattering nationally, and communities throughout the country are facing the challenges presented by a new, quickly growing immigrant population.

The Hispanic population is characterized by a youthful age structure; a large number of foreign born, including many "undocumented"; low levels of education; and disproportionate concentration in low-skill, low-wage jobs. And its presence is being felt in the nation's schools, labor market, health care systems, and political life. A pivotal element of this story is the Hispanic second generation, the children of Spanish-speaking immigrants, who are coming of age as the white majority population is aging. Now numbering 10 million, the second generation is projected to grow to 26 million over the next 25 years. Today the majority of the second generation is in school; by 2030 the majority will be in the labor force. Their economic and social integration will depend on educational investments made today:

the Hispanic demographic dividend can be harnessed for the benefit not only of future generations of Hispanics, but also of the nation.

HISPANIC IDENTITY

Despite their common language and ancestral ties to Spain, Hispanics are highly diverse. Altogether they represent 20 Spanish-speaking nationalities, both recent immigrants and families that date back to the first Spanish settlements in what is now the United States. Differences by generation, legal status, and nationality affect many dimensions of their social integration, but foreign birth and legal status are the most decisive because they reflect differences in English proficiency, educational attainment, and familiarity with U.S. institutions.

"Hispanics" do not exist in Latin America and the Spanish-speaking Caribbean. Coined as an ethnic category in the mid-1970s by government regulation, the U.S.-made panethnic term gained popular currency after being used in the 1980 census short form and in all subsequent Census Bureau surveys and censuses. The term "Latino"—most popular in California during the 1980s and 1990s—was added to the 2000 census. Often used interchangeably, both terms are widely contested, with no consensus on their full meaning. If U.S. Hispanics are forced to choose between the panethnic terms, Hispanic is preferred to Latino by a margin of 3 to 1.

Routine use of both labels for classification purposes has gradually transformed the terms from ethnic categories into racial identities, especially among the second generation. Thus, rather than viewing themselves as an ethnic group, growing numbers of Hispanics are beginning to view themselves as a separate race. The move away from white identity among second-generation Hispanics stands in strong contrast to the experience of earlier immigrant groups from southern and Eastern Europe, whose social acceptance and cultural assimilation in the United States involved self-identification as white. The key question for the future is whether Hispanicity will evolve into a symbolic identity for some or all people of Latin American descent as they join the American mainstream, or whether it will become an enduring marker of disadvantaged minority group status.

SOCIAL INTEGRATION AND MOBILITY

With time, most immigrant communities become ethnic groups, and within three generations (i.e., the grandchildren of immigrants) most expressions of ethnicity are rendered symbolic as a result of intermarriage, acquired proficiency in English, improved socioeconomic status, and residence in ethnically integrated neighborhoods. Hispanic immigrant communities are experiencing this assimilation process. Most notable are the pace of language shift and intermarriage trends—two pillars of socioeconomic integration and Americanization. Hispanic intermarriage with whites, which is most common among those who are U.S. born and who are better educated, increases socioeconomic mobility.

Areas densely populated by Hispanics, especially by recent immigrants, give the impression that the United States is becoming a bilingual nation. The seeming ubiquity of Spanish in these neighborhoods is, in reality, a transitory phenomenon reflecting the large number of recent immigrants. For Hispanics, Spanish fluency erodes the longer immigrants are in this country and across generations. As did prior non-English-speaking immigrant groups, Hispanics are experiencing a decline in their use of, preference for, and fluency in Spanish. Recent trends suggest that the grandchildren of the present wave of immigrants will likely be primarily English monolingual.

Trends in wages, household income, wealth, and home ownership across time and generations point to the gradual ascension of many U.S.-born Hispanics to the middle class. But as a group Hispanics are losing economic ground relative to whites because of the weak economic position of large numbers of low-skilled immigrants, many of whom are undocumented, which lowers the population averages on socioeconomic measures.

In contrast to these important similarities with previous immigrant groups, several important features distinguish the Hispanic experience from those of other ethnic and minority groups. Understanding these differences is essential for appreciating the opportunities that the growing numbers of Hispanics represent for their communities and for the nation, as well as for alerting policy makers of potential risks to the nation's economic and political life.

First, a very large proportion of Hispanics—almost half—are foreign born, among whom roughly 40 percent are undocumented. Given the dominance in this group of Mexicans who come to this country with low levels of formal schooling, foreign-born Hispanics feature both high employment and high poverty rates. Hampered by their limited education and a lack of English skills, Hispanic immigrants are concentrated in low-skilled service-sector, agriculture, and production jobs that pay low average wages. That many undocumented workers experience wage discrimination further depresses the earnings of the foreign born.

Second, unlike the wave of European immigration that ebbed following World War I, immigration from Latin America has continued at high levels for three decades. Since 1950, the Hispanic population has increased from 4 million to more than 40 million. During the 1980s and 1990s, the increase was driven by immigration from Latin America and the Caribbean. During the current decade and for the future, Hispanic growth from births is projected to eclipse that from immigration. However, immigration—both legal and illegal—is likely to remain at high levels for at least another generation. At the same time, fertility rates for Hispanics are above those of the native white population. These demographic processes concentrate the swelling numbers of Hispanics in the first and second generations, precisely those facing the formidable challenges of integration.

Third, changes in the U.S. economy since the mid-1970s that increased demand for skilled workers—precisely when the Hispanic population began to expand—magnify the difficulties they face in joining the U.S. mainstream. As a relatively young population with low average education levels, Hispanics are overrepresented in the types of low-skill jobs that have experienced significant wage erosion in recent decades. Despite improvements in job skills over time and across generations for Hispanics, the sustained influx of immigrants with limited education maintains the population's strong presence in low-wage jobs.

Fourth, unlike prior waves of European immigrants and even of most Latin American immigrants who arrived before 1990, recent Hispanic arrivals are less likely to settle in traditional gateway cities like Los Angeles, New York or Chicago. Lured by intense job growth and the promise of affordable housing, Hispanics are dispersing across the mainland, adding complexity to the long-standing struggle for black-white racial integration as newcomers from Mexico and Central and South America alter the ethnic and racial landscape, forcing multiculturalism in places previously familiar only with black and white. Whether and how the Hispanicization of metropolitan and nonmetropolitan America redraws spatial color lines is an unanswered question with far-reaching implications for social integration and civic engagement. This very new phenomenon and mixed evidence about the reception experiences of new Hispanic immigrants makes it difficult to forecast its effects.

UNCERTAIN FUTURES

By 2030, 25 percent of U.S. residents will be of retirement age or older, but Hispanics are a youthful population. In 2000, their median age was just 27, compared with 39 for non-Hispanic whites. Furthermore, today the median age of the Hispanic second generation, the nation's future workers, is just over 12. Rising numbers of Hispanic young people will slow the nation's overall population aging and can partially offset the growing burden of dependency produced by an aging majority. But their success in doing so depends on the level of their earnings, which in turn depends on their education and acquisition of job-related skills. Currently, Hispanics' representation among highly skilled U.S. workers is below the national average.

Perhaps the most profound risk facing Hispanics is failure to graduate from high school, which remains unacceptably high. The share of Hispanic high school students 16 to 19 years old who failed to graduate fell only marginally during the 1990s, from 22 to 21 percent. Foreign-born Hispanic youths 16 to 19 years old are significantly more likely than native-born students to drop out of high school—34 compared with 14 percent in 2000—but being foreign born is not the main reason that they fail to graduate. Many immigrant students who drop out are recent arrivals who were already behind in school before arriving in the United States. In addition, in the urban schools that many Hispanics attend, low graduation rates are typical. Fully 40 percent of Hispanic students attend high schools that serve large numbers of low-income minority students and graduate less than 60 percent of entering freshmen.

Hispanic college enrollment is on the rise, but still lags well behind that of whites. In 2000 Hispanics accounted for 11 percent of high school graduates, but only 7 percent of students enrolled in 4-year institutions and 14 percent of enrollees in 2-year schools. Hispanic students are more likely than whites to attend 2-year colleges, which decreases the likelihood that they will complete a bachelor's degree. As a result, the Hispanic-white college gap is increasing, despite the fact that Hispanic college enrollment is on the rise.

Hispanic students who fail to master English before leaving school incur considerable costs. English proficiency is mandatory for success in the labor market and is vitally important for navigating health care systems and for meaningful civic engagement. How to ensure proficiency in English remains highly controversial: there is no consensus on how best to teach non-English-speaking students across the grade spectrum.

The significance of Hispanics' high school dropout rates, low enrollment rates in 4-year colleges, and need to master English cannot be overstated because the fastest-growing and best-paying jobs now require at least some postsecondary education. In 1999, nearly 6 of 10 jobs required college-level skills, including many that had not required college training in the past. In rapidly growing occupations, such as health services, nearly three in four jobs now require some college education. These trends bode ill for Hispanics as their college attendance and graduation gap with whites widens.

Additional challenges for Hispanics are posed by new developments that affect families and children. The number of Hispanic mother-only families is growing, as it is for other ethnic and racial groups. Because mother-only families are significantly more likely to be poor, this trend signals heightened vulnerabilities for a growing number of youth. Moreover, it is too soon to tell what the long-term effects of welfare reform will be on Hispanics—especially on groups that rely most heavily on public benefits.

Young people are also at risk of failure because of the rising numbers of Hispanic families that lack health insurance. Expansions of federally subsidized programs such as Medicaid and the State Children's Health Insurance Program appear unlikely in an era of unprecedented federal budget deficits. Continued immigration of Hispanics from Mexico and other countries in Central and South America, coupled with their geographic dispersal to areas unaccustomed to providing care for diverse groups of patients, will challenge current approaches to providing health insurance coverage and health care to low-income Hispanics, particularly to recent immigrants.

There are also troublesome signs of declining health among Hispanic children, signaled by elevated levels of risk for diabetes, atherosclerosis, and cardiovascular disease, along with increasing rates of obesity and its myriad complications. For the burgeoning second generation, the implications of this trend are ominous, especially in light of the number of children who do not receive preventive care because they lack health care coverage.

With institutional investments, Hispanic immigrants and their children can acquire the education and language skills necessary to realize the Hispanic demographic dividend, namely the higher earning potential of a youthful Hispanic workforce. In 2000 the 2-year average educational gap between all Hispanics and whites cost about $100 billion in lost earnings.

Given the growth in the Hispanic populations that is projected to occur over the next 30 years, the cost of this education gap could rise to $212 billion in current dollars by 2030, taking into account the generational shift.

Failure to close Hispanics' education and language gaps risks compromising their ability to both contribute to and share in national prosperity. How these risks and opportunities play out over the decades ahead will define not only the kind of future Hispanics will inherit, but also the economic and social contours of the United States in the 21st century.

Julio Valdez
Personaje con Historia (2001)
Copyright by the artist; used with permission of Julio Valdez Studio.

1

Introduction

A s the U.S. population approaches the 300 million mark, Hispanics—who presently number more than 40 million residents—are entering a crucial phase in their long and complex history. As a result of both continuing immigration and natural increase, the Hispanic population is growing by more than 1.5 million annually.[1] Today Hispanics make up approximately 13 percent of the total U.S. population. In 2030, nearly 1 in 4 U.S. residents will be Hispanic, up from nearly 1 in 7 in 2005. Over time, many Hispanics lose their individual nation-based identities through both intermarriage and a shift in their perceptions of themselves.[2]

Past waves of immigrants from Latin America and the Caribbean fueled Hispanic population growth during the last two decades of the 20th century, and while immigration is still a potent force behind the numbers, today the children and grandchildren of immigrants are spurring the increase. The growth of these second- and third-generation Hispanics, their socioeconomic diversification, their increasing geographic dispersal, and their entitlements as U.S.-born citizens will have major social, economic, cultural, and political impacts on the nation between now and midcentury—impacts that will be intensified by the simultaneous aging of the larger white population. Growing numbers of Hispanics are finishing school, entering the labor market, joining health care systems, and becoming engaged in local and national political arenas, while also helping to refashion consumer markets.

s are coming of age in an aging society has important
nation's future. As the youngest segment of the U.S.
nd third-generation Hispanics could play a vital role
den of a graying society. Yet realizing this potential
depend on whether the necessary educational in-
n investments will determine whether these young
e sufficient human capital—literacy, education, and job
o gain access to higher-skilled jobs and avail themselves of new
opportunities for social inclusion. Also crucial will be new social policies
that both promote their integration into social and political institutions
and foster greater equity in economic arenas.

An emphasis in this report, then, is on the potential costs of
underinvesting in the young Hispanic population, as well as the perils of
allowing a large and growing undocumented population to live on the
fringes of society. There currently exists a rising skill gap between Hispanics
and whites. Although this gap is largely the product of the sizable number
of low-skill immigrants, schooling trends among the native born contribute to it. Even as the number of Hispanic college graduates has reached an
all-time high, thousands of native-born Hispanic youths are failing to complete high school. The high premium on skill in today's labor market will
magnify the deleterious consequences of Hispanics' low educational attainment in the future. Indeed, low levels of formal schooling and poor English
proficiency account for the large number of Hispanics in service-sector
jobs, as well as their low average wages, relatively poor health status, and
weak civic engagement.

This report is the product of a 2-year study by a panel of experts convened by the National Academies and supported by several foundations
and U.S. government agencies. This panel was charged with conducting a
study of the significant demographic changes taking place among the U.S.
Hispanic population and their progress relative to the mainstream in several key areas. The panel could also consider ways to improve related data
collection. The main purpose of the report is to help inform future policy
debate and provide government, public institutions, and the private sector
with the information needed to allocate resources for the enduring benefit
of both the Hispanic population and the nation as a whole.

In the edited volume *Hispanics and the Future of America* that serves as
the companion to this report, readers will find a more detailed review of
Hispanics' history, demography, geography, education, family, employment,

economic well-being, health, and political engagement. That information provided much of the evidence for the discussion in this report. Appendix A describes the panel's additional activities and statistical sources consulted.[3] Biographical sketches of panel members and staff are provided in Appendix B and contents of the companion volume *Hispanics and the Future of America* are in Appendix C.

The report is organized as follows. Chapter 2 presents a review of the origins of Hispanics in the United States, their patterns of immigration, and the demographic and political forces that have shaped them as a minority group, as well as a contemporary demographic profile. It describes how Hispanics joined Native Americans in what is now the United States and how they came to become immigrants in their own land, and considers the contributions of immigration and fertility to the current growth and diversification of the Hispanic population, including the sizable numbers who remain undocumented. The issue of legal status is examined in some detail.

Chapter 3 reviews the origins of the "Hispanic" identity and examines self-identity and language/linguistic assimilation among Hispanics today. It also considers such questions as whether there is in fact a unique Hispanic identity and whether Hispanics are a separate race. Finally, the chapter indicates how data on the Hispanic population can be improved.

Chapter 4 addresses the challenges of social, economic, and political integration in the context of rising inequality, the growing trend among Hispanics to settle in locales beyond their traditional areas of residence, and patterns of Hispanic civic engagement. It identifies important ways in which Hispanics differ from earlier immigrant groups with emphasis on contextual issues, notably contemporary economic conditions and the aging majority population.

Chapter 5 examines four key dimensions of the Hispanic experience: family and living arrangements, schools and education, economic well-being, and health status and access to care. The discussion highlights the risks and opportunities whose outcomes will shape the future of Hispanics in the United States.

The uncertainties associated with the risks and opportunities identified in Chapter 6 are conveyed by the title of the final chapter—"Uncertain Destinies." Will Hispanics realize increased economic well-being and a greater political voice, allowing them to share fully in the nation's prosperity? One certainty is emphasized: that the potential demographic dividend of the labor market participation of the youthful Hispanic population, as well as Hispanics' social and economic future, will be compromised by underinvestment in the education of their second generation.

NOTES

1 U.S. Bureau of the Census, 2005. This estimate does not include the 4 million residents of Puerto Rico, although they are U.S. citizens.

2 Given a choice, migrants from Latin America overwhelmingly prefer to self-identify by country of origin, but if forced to choose between the two panethnic terms, they prefer "Hispanic" to "Latino" by a margin of three to one. "Black" and "white," as used herein, refer to non-Hispanic African Americans/blacks and whites.

3 There are areas in which data are emerging that the report does not cover; criminal justice, religion, and the military are three such examples. The panel considered these topics but decided that the research base was inadequate to build strong conclusions.

Kathy Vargas
Este Recuerdo (2001)
Copyright by the artist; used with permission.

2

Multiple Origins, Hispanic Portrait

Hispanics are a highly diverse population representing 20 Spanish-speaking nationalities as well as some of the earliest settlements in what is now the United States. Differences among these groups in social and economic status, political behavior, and health magnify their diversity, as discussed in Chapter 3. The dramatic increase over the past 50 years in the size of the Hispanic population has been driven by a combination of immigration and births. Today nearly half are foreign-born, many among them undocumented. These demographic dimensions of the Hispanic population are significant for Hispanics' social, economic, and political integration in the United States (discussed in Chapter 5).

In 1950, approximately 4 million Hispanics lived in the United States, most of them in California, Texas, New York, and Florida. By 2004 there were more than 40 million—a 900 percent increase in half a century—scattered throughout the country. (See Chapter 4 for a discussion of the dispersal of the Hispanic population.) Hispanics share a language, origins on two continents, and, since the mid-19th century, an immigration history. Yet, there is enormous diversity among nationality groups. Together, eight countries—Mexico, El Salvador, Guatemala, Cuba, the Dominican Republic, Colombia, Peru, and Ecuador—plus Puerto Rico account for some 90 percent of all U.S. Hispanics. The remainder have their origins in Honduras, Costa Rica, Nicaragua, Panama, Argentina, Bolivia, Chile, Paraguay, Uruguay, Venezuela, and Spain. Hispanics also include those long-term natives who can trace their roots back centuries, long before the United

19

States became a sovereign nation. Mexicans and their descendants far out-number any other Hispanic group—over 60 percent of those who identify themselves as "Hispanic" or "Latino" are of Mexican origin. In fact, the sheer numbers of people of Mexican origin—22.3 million in 2000—render generalizations about the Hispanic population problematic as they may in fact be characterizing the experience of Mexicans—a group dominated by large numbers of low-skilled, low-income immigrants.[1]

Excluded from the Hispanic rubric are Latin Americans who are not Spanish speaking, notably English- and French-speaking Guyanese and Dutch-speaking Surinamese. Brazilians also are not Hispanic—and do not consider themselves to be—although they are Latin American.[2] In general, moreover, Portuguese-speaking people originating in Portugal and Brazil are excluded from the Hispanic category, which evolved from the Spanish-origin and Spanish-language population constructs used in 1970 by the U.S. government (as discussed below).

Currently, more Hispanics reside in the United States and its territories than in Colombia—the largest Spanish-speaking country in South America—or in Spain itself. Only Mexico, with a population exceeding 100 million, has a larger Hispanic population than the United States.

In contrast to other ethnic groups in the United States, Hispanics are both an indigenous and an immigrant community. Indeed, the Spanish roots of the United States are actually older than those of any other European group, antedating by over a century the creation of a permanent English colony in North America. No understanding of the contemporary Hispanic population can ignore its historical and geographic roots. The indelible imprint of these roots remains evident even today across the southern rim of the United States, from San Diego to Sarasota.

HISPANIC ROOTS

The Spanish origins of what is now the United States date to 1513, when Juan Ponce de León first explored *La Florida*.[3] Spain claimed much of the American south and the entire southwest—at least half of the present U.S. mainland—and governed these areas for well over two centuries, a period longer than the United States has existed as an independent nation.

By the time of the American Revolution in the late 1700s, Spain's cultural reach extended from San Diego to San Francisco on the west coast; throughout the southwest from Tucson to Santa Fé, El Paso, and San Antonio; along the Mississippi River from St. Louis to New Orleans; and east-ward through towns that stretched to Florida's Atlantic coast by way of Mobile, Pensacola, and Tallahassee. The names of thousands of locales, from Sacramento to Cape Cañaveral—including several states—attest to the nation's Spanish beginnings.

In 1848, the Mexican War ended with the United States expanding its territory by a million square miles while severing nearly half of Mexico's. At the conclusion of the Spanish-American War in 1898, Spain ceded its last colony, Puerto Rico, to the United States in the Treaty of Paris, which consolidated the status of the United States as a global power. The peoples of the conquered territories, some of whom were native to the land now called the United States, were subjected to laws and practices similar to the Jim Crow apartheid system that discriminated against blacks after the Civil War. Rooted most deeply in Texas, these injustices caused U.S.-born Mexican Americans living in the Southwest to see themselves as foreigners in their own country.

Since the end of the 19th century, Mexicans have been the dominant Hispanic group living in the United States. When, in 1848, the Treaty of Guadalupe-Hidalgo ceded the lands of the Southwest to the United States, there were perhaps 75,000 inhabitants of Mexican origin residing in that vast territory—nearly three-fourths of them (called "Hispanos") in New Mexico, with smaller numbers living in Texas ("Tejanos") and California ("Californios"). Until the Civil Rights era, these Mexican Americans, especially those in Texas, endured pervasive social and economic discrimination, reflected, e.g., in segregated schools, churches, and residential neighborhoods.[4]

In the 1910 census, Mexicans numbered some 220,000—a figure that more than doubled by 1920 and trebled a decade later, when the U.S. Bureau of the Census classified Mexicans as a separate race. By the early 1900s, railroad lines linked the interior of Mexico with Texas and other states, shuttling significant numbers of Mexican laborers to the copper and coal mines of Arizona and Colorado and the steel mills and slaughterhouses of Chicago, Detroit, and Pittsburgh. By 2000, more than 22 million Hispanics of Mexican descent were living in the United States—a striking increase over the 8.7 million counted in the 1980 census.

Along with Mexicans, Puerto Ricans and Cubans formed the Hispanic mosaic in the United States until a few decades ago. Whereas Mexicans settled largely in five Southwestern states (California, Texas, Arizona, New

Mexico, and Colorado), Puerto Ricans lived in the Northeast (in particular New York City), while Cubans lived mainly in south Florida and the New York/New Jersey region.

Puerto Ricans are U.S. citizens and therefore are free to travel and settle on the U.S. mainland. Some 3.5 million Puerto Ricans resided on the mainland in 2000, making them the nation's second-largest Hispanic group.[5] At the end of World War II, high unemployment in Puerto Rico, combined with inexpensive airfares, boosted travel between San Juan and New York City, making Puerto Ricans the first airborne migrants in U.S. history. Most of the early migrants settled in the East Harlem area of New York City, while far smaller numbers populated urban neighborhoods in Chicago, Detroit, and other northern cities. Although Puerto Ricans have begun settling in new enclaves outside the barrios of the northeast, in 2000 there were still twice as many Puerto Ricans living in New York (more than 850,000) as in San Juan. Roughly half of all Puerto Ricans live on the mainland, the other half on the island.

Like other former Spanish colonies, Cuba did not escape a turbulent past. As Spanish rule became more repressive, and after the Ten Years War broke out in 1868, Cubans began emigrating, first to New York and later to Florida. Many of these new arrivals had been successful business owners in Cuba and represented a new class of Latin American immigrants in the United States. A much larger wave of Cuban immigrants—political refugees—began arriving in Florida when, in 1959, Fidel Castro overthrew Fulgencio Batista. From the first waves of the 1960s, to the Marielitos of 1980, to the *balseros* (rafters) of the 1990s, successive waves of Cuban exiles have established a sizable presence in Florida, their visibility magnified by their residential concentration in the Miami area. In 2000, Cuban-origin Hispanics numbered 1.3 million—a significant increase of 1.2 million over their 1960 population of just 70,000. Cuban transplants have even recreated their homeland in Little Havana, a Miami enclave reminiscent of pre-Castro Cuba. As growing numbers of Central Americans and Puerto Ricans relocate to Florida, Cubans continue to enjoy political power and economic dominance and maintain a distinctive voice within the Hispanic community.

A CONTEMPORARY PROFILE

In the summer of 2003, the Census Bureau announced that the U.S. Hispanic population, numbering just shy of 39 million in April of that year, had edged out non-Hispanic blacks as the nation's largest minority population.[6] Moreover, Hispanics were now the country's fastest-growing ethnic minority—increasing at a rate 4 times faster than the total population and 14 times faster than that of whites.[7]

Several features distinguish the Hispanic population from African Americans. First is the diversity noted earlier. Second, nearly half of all Hispanics living in the United States today were born elsewhere, including the sizable number that are undocumented. Finally, Hispanics are a particularly youthful population: in 2000, their median age was just 27.

In 1960, when the baby boom swelled the U.S. population to 186 million, Hispanics accounted for a mere 4 percent of the total—just under 7 million. By 2000, 1 of every 7 U.S. residents self-identified as "Hispanic" or "Latino" in the census. Persons of Mexican, Puerto Rican, and Cuban descent currently represent 77 percent of the Hispanic population. Dominicans and those who trace their roots to one of the Spanish-speaking countries of Central or South America, or to Spain itself, make up the remaining 23 percent.

Hispanics are the largest foreign-born population in the country—a milestone reached in 1990 when, for the first time, immigration from Latin America exceeded the combined flows from Asia and Europe. By 2000, Mexican immigrants alone were more numerous than all European and Canadian immigrants together, and more than all Asian, African, and Middle Eastern immigrants combined.

Sustaining the growth of the Hispanic population today are both the extremely high flows of Latin American immigrants into the United States and the traditionally high Hispanic birth rates. Among Hispanics in the United States, 1 in 2 was born abroad (compared with 1 in 13 non-Hispanics), and approximately 1 in 3 (31 percent) is a member of a rapidly growing second generation—the U.S.-born children of immigrant parents.

Over time, the relative contribution of immigration and births to the growth of the Hispanic population has shifted. During the 1960s, when the Hispanic population increased by 3.9 million, births outpaced immigrants by about 2 to 1. In the following decade, the two components of growth were nearly equal—approximately 3 million each, with a slight edge for births. During the last two decades, however, immigration has outpaced fertility as the leading component of Hispanic population growth: in the 1980s, 5.5 million immigrants from Latin America and the Caribbean were added to the Hispanic population, compared with 4.4 million Hispanic

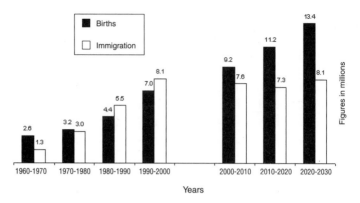

FIGURE 2-1 Hispanic births and net immigration by decade: 1960-1970 to 2020-2030.
SOURCE: Passel (2004).

births, while the 1990s added 8 million immigrants and 7 million births (see Figure 2-1).

Traditionally, Hispanics have big families (see Chapter 5). Currently, the typical Mexican, Puerto Rican, or "other Hispanic" woman bears about one more child than the typical white woman.[8] Cuban women are an exception, having a fertility rate nearly identical to that of whites. This difference is due partly to the older average age at which Cuban women begin having children—older than women from other Hispanic subgroups, placing them past their prime reproductive years—and partly to their higher levels of education and rates of labor force participation. More-educated men and women have fewer children. On average, immigrant Mexican, Central American, and Dominican women complete only primary or middle school, but most Cuban women hold high school diplomas or complete some college, which prompts many to postpone marriage and childbearing in order to begin careers.

Over the past 20 years Hispanics have experienced the trend toward increased nonmarital childbearing that has been documented for the general U.S. population, with notable variation by subgroup. In 2000 Cubans were closer to whites (27 percent and 22 percent of births to unmarried mothers respectively), while Puerto Ricans were closer to blacks (59 percent and 69 percent of births to unmarried mothers, respectively). Mexicans and Central and South Americans fell between the extremes, with 41 percent and 44 percent of births to unmarried mothers respectively.

While nonmarital childbearing has increased for all groups, there was a substantial decrease in the percentage of births to young teen mothers for almost all groups between 1980 and 2000. However, the decline was smaller for most Hispanic subgroups compared with whites and blacks. In 2000, Mexican, Puerto Rican, and other Hispanic infants were more likely than Cuban and Central/South American infants to have a teenage mother. The figures for the former groups are more similar to that of blacks, while those for the latter are similar to that of whites.[9]

Foreign-born Hispanic women have higher fertility than their native-born counterparts and non-Hispanic women. In the second generation Hispanic women's fertility drops significantly. For example, on average, second-generation Mexican women have 2.1 children, while immigrant Mexican women have 2.7.[10] Intergenerational increases in educational attainment for women seem to account for some of the decline in Mexican women's fertility across generations.

Although in recent years immigration has edged out fertility as the chief component of Hispanic population growth, the reverse may soon be true because of the swelling second generation resulting from immigrant fertility. If it is assumed that immigration will continue its current gradual increase, births are likely to surpass immigration as the principal component driving Hispanic population growth because the number of Hispanic women of childbearing age will have grown significantly.[11] This scenario is probable even with the declining birth rates of U.S.-born Hispanic women compared to immigrant Hispanic women. As Figure 2-1 shows, this source of demographic momentum is projected to continue well into the current century. After 2020, the ratio of births to immigrants per decade should approximate the proportions attained in the 1960s—nearly 2:1—except that the absolute numbers added will be more than five times larger: 21 million versus 4 million persons added to the population every 10 years.[12]

Given the influence of immigration in the rapid compounding of the Hispanic population, it is interesting to speculate how the U.S. population would look had national borders been sealed to all immigration after 1960. This exercise also illustrates the extent to which immigration has contributed to the size of the Hispanic population. Figure 2-2 shows a projected comparison of the growth in the total U.S. and Hispanic populations with and without the immigration that has occurred (taking into consideration new arrivals and new births to foreign-born women and their children).[13] This projection shows that since 1960, immigrants and their offspring have added approximately 47 million residents to the total U.S. population—

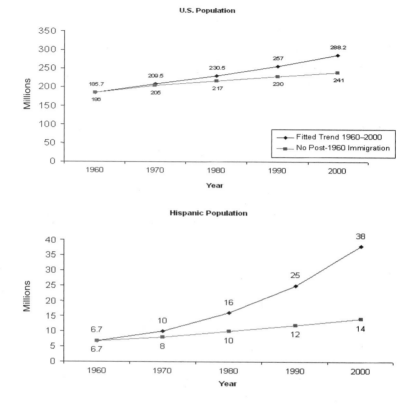

FIGURE 2-2 Projected U.S. and Hispanic population without immigration: 1960 to 2000.
SOURCE: Passel (2004).

less than half of the total increase. However, immigration and the fertility of foreign-born women have increased the Hispanic population by more than 170 percent. Thus, had the United States closed its borders to immigrants after 1960, the Hispanic population would have been much smaller—a mere 14 million versus the projected 38 million—and would account for only 6 percent of 241 million U.S. residents rather than 13 percent of 288 million.

Immigration and birth rates vary among Hispanic subgroups and by social class, generation, and legal status. Foreign-born Mexicans doubled their numbers between the 1990 and 2000 censuses, while other subgroups, although smaller in absolute size, grew at even faster rates. As a result of the violence and civil unrest in Central America during the 1980s, immigrant Salvadorans, Guatemalans, and Nicaraguans tripled their numbers in the United States in the 1990s. The number of foreign-born Dominicans, Peruvians, and Bolivians doubled in the 1980s, and then doubled again in the 1990s. New migrant streams such as these generally portend increased momentum of immigration because once established, immigrant social networks provide a powerful impetus for future flows. These circumstances also contribute to the growth of undocumented immigration.

LEGAL STATUS

A distinctive feature of Hispanic immigration is the large and growing number of undocumented immigrants. The best contemporary estimate is that close to 11 million undocumented migrants resided in the United States in 2005, 80 percent of them from Mexico and other Latin American countries.[14] Mexicans alone account for 57 percent of the entire undocumented population, and more than 80 percent of all Mexican immigrants who arrived in the United States after 1990 were undocumented.[15] For perspective, the number of undocumented residents in the United States is larger than the populations of some Latin American countries, such as Uruguay, Paraguay, Nicaragua, El Salvador, or Costa Rica.

Many decades in the making, undocumented Hispanic immigration is in part a consequence of both employer demand for cheap, hardworking laborers and failed immigration policy (see Table 2-1).[16] Primarily at the behest of American growers, immigration laws in 1921 and 1924 that were designed to exclude immigrants from Asia, Africa, and nonwestern Europe explicitly exempted persons from Mexico, Cuba, Haiti, the Dominican Republic, the Canal Zone, and the independent countries of Central and South America from the numerical quotas.[17] This conveniently permitted unregulated recruitment of Mexican workers as needed and their prompt deportation when they were not, as occurred during the 1930s when about 400,000 (including, as it happened, many U.S. citizens) were repatriated to Mexico. During the mid-1950s, Operation Wetback resulted in the repatriation of even larger numbers of Mexicans—again, legal residents and U.S. citizens among them.[18]

Several other factors have contributed to the intense flow of undocumented immigration from Mexico. First, the termination in 1964 of the Bracero Accords, which authorized a binational agricultural guestworker program, signaled the closing of an important labor safety valve precisely at

TABLE 2-1 Selected Immigration Legislation in the United States

Year	Legislation	Content
1924	National Origins Act	Created a system of national quotas that restricted immigration to 2 percent of national origin groups as of 1890.
1940	Alien Registration Act	Advocated by Senator Joseph McCarthy, required the registration and fingerprinting of all aliens, and enforced laws regarding immigration and deportation.
1952	Immigration and Nationality Act (McCarran-Walter)	Reinstated the national origins quota system of 1924, and limited total annual immigration to one-sixth of 1 percent of the 1920 continental population. Extended the right of naturalization to all races.
1965	Immigration and Nationality Act (Hart-Celler)	Granted priority to family reunification and repealed the national origins quota system.
1978	Worldwide Ceiling Law	A combination ceiling of both Eastern and Western Hemispheres totaling 290,000. It also extended the 20,000 per country maximum to Western Hemisphere countries.
1980	Refugee Act	Established to harbor people fleeing Vietnam; granted asylum to politically oppressed refugees.
1986	Immigration Reform and Control Act	Sanctioned employers who hired undocumented workers; granted amnesty to approximately 3 million undocumented residents.
1990	Immigration Act	Promoted immigration, particularly for highly skilled professionals.
1996	Illegal Immigration Reform and Immigrant Responsibility Act	Increased criminal penalties for immigration-related offenses, authorized increases in enforcement personnel, enhanced enforcement authority, and made immigrant sponsorship legally enforceable.
1998	American Competitiveness and Workforce Improvement Act	Increased H-1B visa quotas from 1999 to 2002 for skilled information technology workers. H-1B visas allow foreign nationals with special skills to work in the United States.

TABLE 2-1 Continued

Year	Legislation	Content
2000	American Competitiveness in the 21st Century Act	Raised the annual limit for H-1Bs in fiscal years 2000 through 2003 from the previous 115,000 to 195,000.
2000	Legal Immigration and Family Equity Act	Permitted the reunion of families long separated by delays in the processing of immigrant visas.
2001	Extension of 245(i) of the Immigration and Nationality Act	Allows immigrants who entered the United States without inspection or who overstayed their visas to adjust their status to lawful permanent residence without having to leave the United States, provided they pay a $1,000 penalty and are beneficiaries of family- or employment-based visa petitions filed on or before a certain date.
2001	Patriot Act	Broadened the grounds for excluding terrorists and aliens with ties to terrorist organizations and detaining immigrants thought to be involved in terrorist activities.
2002	Border Security and Visa Reform Act	Increased the number of Immigration and Naturalization Service (INS) personnel and authorized appropriations for INS, Border Patrol, and consular personnel, training, facilities, and security-related technology.

SOURCES: Jasso and Resenzweig (1990) and Kuck (2005).

a time that demographic and economic pressures were mounting in Mexico. Many immigrants went through the process of legalization with the help of their employers. Others, planning to be in the United States only temporarily, decided not to legalize to avoid the bureaucratic delays involved and stayed in the country illegally.

Second, the 1978 amendment to the Hart-Celler Act that tightened requirements for legally authorized immigration from Mexico inadvertently increased pressure for undocumented entry into the United States to skirt the requirements. Finally, legislation designed to curb the flow of undocu-

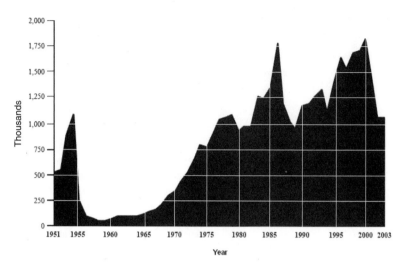

FIGURE 2-3 Apprehensions of undocumented immigrants in the United States, 1951 to 2003.
SOURCE: U.S. Department of Homeland Security (2003).

mented immigrants during the 1980s and 1990s actually had the opposite effect.[19]

Flows of undocumented immigrants peaked in the mid-1980s, declined briefly following the enactment of the 1986 Immigration Reform and Control Act (IRCA), again rose gradually during the 1990s, and then accelerated after the mid-1990s, despite passage of the 1996 Illegal Immigration Reform and Immigrant Responsibility Act (IIRAIRA) (see Figure 2-3). IRCA provided amnesty for undocumented immigrants who met specific residence requirements. It also imposed sanctions on employers who hired undocumented workers and launched what would become a series of initiatives to close the border through various surveillance measures. Ironically, once again, some aspects of the legislation actually encouraged unauthorized migration, particularly from Mexico. For example, provisions that gave growers a 2-day warning prior to labor inspections provided a window for an unabated flow of unauthorized workers that was enabled by the strong social networks among farmworkers.

Additionally, IRCA's amnesty program practically guaranteed future immigration. After adjusting their legal status, legalized immigrants could sponsor husbands and wives, children, parents, and siblings in accordance with the extant visa preference system that authorizes legal immigration. The sheer numbers of undocumented immigrants legalized under IRCA—nearly 3 million, the majority from Latin America—demonstrated that employer sanctions and enhanced border control, which were originally intended to reduce illegal migration flows into the country, had been highly inefficient.

In contrast to IRCA, whose effects generally benefited Hispanics, the 1996 IIRAIRA constituted a serious blow to immigrant communities. Undocumented workers were banned from a wide range of publicly funded support programs and services, including access to in-state college tuition for undocumented youths who graduated from U.S. high schools.[20] Resident immigrants who had work permits but were not citizens also saw their access to social benefits threatened. Ironically, because this was not the intention, by sharpening the divide between legal immigrants and citizens, IIRAIRA triggered an upsurge in naturalization applications. For example, in 1996, the year IIRAIRA was enacted, a record number of Mexican migrants applied for naturalization—triple the number from the year before.[21]

Despite intensified surveillance efforts along the 2000-mile U.S.-Mexican border, which have added another dimension of risk to unlawful entry, and more punitive measures for those who succeed in crossing, the undocumented population continues to grow. The Immigration and Naturalization Service (now U.S. Citizenship and Immigration Services of the Department of Homeland Security) estimated net annual undocumented immigration at 350,000 immigrants during the 1990s, but the Census Bureau and others estimate the number at almost half a million per year, on average.[22] For the most part, undocumented immigrants reside in a handful of states, although there are signs this may be changing. Currently, undocumented immigrants make up more than 40 percent of the foreign-born population in 10 states.[23] Clandestine crossings along the southern border involving Mexicans and Central Americans are responsible for more than half of the continued flow, but the remainder become undocumented by overstaying tourist visas.

The key lesson to be learned from the persistent growth in the size of the undocumented U.S. population is that restrictive immigration policies have repeatedly proven ineffective in sealing the southern border in the face of strong social networks that overcome all sorts of physical and legal barriers to finding jobs.[24] Human ingenuity makes quick work of barriers erected between willing workers and employers hungry for cheap labor. Sanctions against employers who hire undocumented workers have proven ineffective in stemming the tide of workers who readily fill low-wage, low-skill jobs largely because they have not been enforced.

Formidable social risks await the large numbers of undocumented Hispanics forced to live in the shadows of mainstream America. Negative public perceptions of undocumented workers stigmatize legitimate low-wage Hispanic workers by conflating their social and legal status, and since September 11, 2001, associating illegal status with criminal status. Such views also compromise the life chances of the U.S.-born children of the undocumented. National boundaries are rendered meaningless in complex families in which some members are citizens and others are undocumented. The problems U.S.-born children of undocumented immigrants confront dramatize the social and economic risks of illegal status, and particularly the asymmetries between the children and their parents.[25]

In the United States, about 10 percent of children live in households in which at least one parent is a noncitizen and one child is a citizen. Legislation limiting the rights and benefits of noncitizen adults disadvantages these children, who are among the nation's poorest as well. For example, children living with noncitizen parents constitute about a fifth of children nationwide who are uninsured. In addition, both legal and illegal noncitizen parents may be reluctant to approach public or publicly funded institutions for services, despite their children's citizenship and eligibility.[26] The result is that children of immigrants use public benefits less often than children of natives, despite higher rates of economic hardship.[27]

CONCLUSION

The Hispanic population in the United States, highly diverse in its origins, today represents the nation's largest and fastest-growing minority, one characterized by a particularly youthful age structure. Its growth is fueled by both immigration and high fertility.

A large and growing number of undocumented immigrants is another distinctive feature of the Hispanic population. Against the reality of the need for and supply of unskilled workers, the social question regarding undocumented migration is not about simply stopping the flow, for its course is dictated largely by intertwined regional economies. Rather, the core questions concern the terms of admission for those who enter legally, the treatment of those who enter and work without the protection of legal status, and whether (and how) the offspring of undocumented workers will gain access to mainstream institutions.

To answer these questions, later chapters consider where Hispanics are positioned in the social mainstream, and their prospects for participating in mainstream American institutions in the nation's current economy. First, however, it is essential to understand how 40 million culturally diverse people from a score of countries came to be classified under the panethnic label "Hispanic." The next chapter addresses this question.

NOTES

1 Although the 2000 U.S. census put the figure at 20.9 million, the adjusted estimate given here includes persons classified as "Hispanic, other" who were born in Mexico or indicated Mexican ancestry but who merely checked "Hispanic" without specifying further. See Appendix A. Statistics based on the 2000 census reported herein are based on adjusted counts.

2 Rumbaut, 2006:5.

3 St. Augustine, Florida, founded in 1565, is the oldest city in the United States.

4 Montejano, 1987.

5 The 4 million Puerto Ricans living on the island are not considered in this report because their social, political, and economic circumstances differ in profound ways from those of their mainland counterparts. For example, the term "Hispanic" has no resonance on the island of Puerto Rico.

6 U.S. Bureau of the Census, 2003.

7 U.S. Bureau of the Census, 2004a.

8 "Other Hispanic" refers collectively to groups other than Cuban, Mexican, and Puerto Rican.

9 Landale et al., 2006.

10 Durand et al., 2006.

11 Suro and Passel, 2003; Passel, 2004.

12 These projections set the level of immigration for 2005-2010 at a little over 7 million. For subsequent periods, continuing increases in immigration are assumed, albeit at relatively low levels—namely 5 percent over each 5-year period in the baseline projections. More details are provided in Passel, 2004.

13 Passel, 2004.

14 Estimates of the undocumented population vary from 8 to 12 million. Annual increases have been revised upward from 350,000 to 500,000 (Passel, 2005). The Center for Immigration Studies claims that half of the 4.3 million increase in the foreign-born population between 2000 and 2004 involves undocumented immigrants and a rising share of Mexicans in the total estimated flow from 28 percent in 2000 to 31 percent in 2004 (Camarota, 2004).

15 Passel, 2005.

16 Massey et al., 2002.

17 Tienda, 2002.

18 Public Broadcasting Service, *The Border.* Available: http://www.pbs.org/kpbs/theborder/index.html [accessed December 5, 2005].

19 Massey et al., 2002.

20 This measure has been abrogated in several states that have passed legislation to override the restriction. See Tienda, 2002.

21 Durand et al., 2006.

22 Immigration and Naturalization Service, 2003; Passel, 2005.

23 Passel, 2005.

24 Massey et al., 2002.

25 Fix and Zimmermann, 2001.

26 Fix and Zimmermann, 2001.

27 Capps et al., 2005.

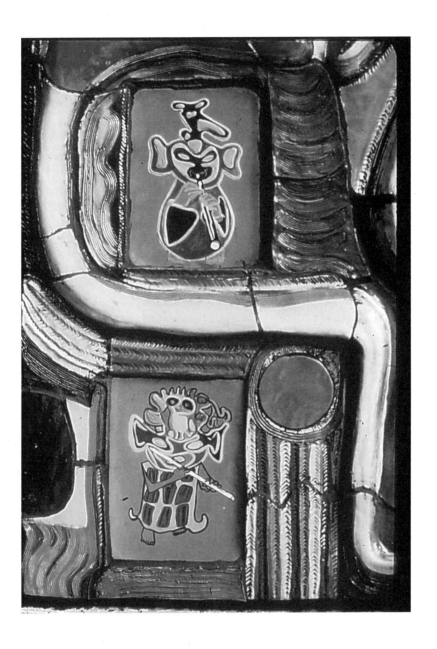

Nitza Tufiño
Taino Symphony (1978)
Copyright by the artist; used with permission.

3

Defining Hispanicity:
E Pluribus Unum or *E Pluribus Plures?*

As immigrants, Hispanics are likely to experience the same social transitions as other immigrant groups. With time, most immigrant communities become ethnic groups, and within three generations (i.e., the grandchildren of the immigrants), most expressions of ethnicity, including language, are rendered symbolic as a result of improved socio-economic status, residence in neighborhoods that are outside of ethnic enclaves, and intermarriage. There are signs that similar processes are occurring among Hispanic communities. However, it is uncertain whether "Hispanic" will evolve to become a symbolic identity for people of Latin American descent who become part of the American mainstream. There are risks that Hispanicity could be an enduring marker of ethnic and minority group status.

As detailed below, the panethnic term "Hispanic" became official government terminology in the mid-1970s.[1] The term gained popular currency after being used in the 1980 census and all subsequent census schedules. It was joined by "Latino"—most popular in California during the 1980s and 1990s—in census 2000.[2] Often used interchangeably, both terms are widely debated. Nor is there consensus on their usage, although there are clear preferences. Given a choice, migrants from Latin America overwhelmingly prefer to self-identify by country of origin, but if required to choose between the two panethnic terms, they prefer "Hispanic" to "Latino" by a margin of 3 to 1.[3] It is worth noting that Hispanics are "Hispanic" only in the United States; in their home countries, the term neither resonates nor is used.

Of greater significance are the meanings signified by both "Hispanic" and "Latino"—terms that mask the enormous diversity of this eclectic population. As noted in Chapter 2, while united by a common ancestral language, Hispanics diverge in a number of respects. These include national origin, social history, legal status, shades of skin color, socioeconomic status, religion, and political views—just about every element that has bound other immigrant groups in the United States.[4] Because nearly half of all Hispanics living in the United States today were born abroad, the Spanish language has proliferated in places where large numbers have settled. Acting as a kind of cultural mortar, the universality of the language has created an illusion of ethnic unity among Hispanics that is belied by their diversity: there is no monolithic Hispanic population with a common history or common problems.

Moreover, it is unclear at this point how enduring Hispanic identity will prove to be beyond the third generation. The extent to which U.S.-born children or grandchildren of recent immigrants from Latin America will consider themselves Hispanic is an open question. Longitudinal studies suggest that only about a quarter of second-generation Hispanics tend to adopt a panethnic identity, although members of this group are much more likely than their parents to accept Hispanic or Latino as a racial (as opposed to ethnic) self-identifier.

ORIGINS OF HISPANIC IDENTITY

Whether the handiwork of legislators or the invention of academics, classification systems create and shape ethnic and racial boundaries. In the aftermath of the Civil Rights movement of the 1960s, new social legislation—in particular, grant-in-aid programs that allocated federal dollars on the basis of population formulas—called for more accurate counts of people of Spanish origin.[5] In response, the word "Hispanic" was adopted by the federal government to denote those who traced their ancestry to Spain, Mexico, and the Spanish-speaking countries of the Caribbean and Central and South America. In 1976, Congress enacted Public Law 94-311, which both defined (and thus created) the Hispanic population and mandated the collection, analysis, and publication of data on that population.

Laws require implementation guidelines. One such guideline, Directive 15, issued in 1977 by the Office of Management and Budget (OMB), standardized the collection and reporting of "racial" and "ethnic" statistics, including data on persons of Spanish/Hispanic origin. Directive 15 not only authorized the term "Hispanic" for official use, but also specified a minimal classification of four "social races," later revised to five—White, Black or African American, Asian, American Indian or Alaska Native, and Native Hawaiian or Other Pacific Islander—and two ethnic backgrounds— "of Hispanic origin" and "not of Hispanic origin."[6] Because the government routinely uses the terms "Hispanic" and "Latino" equivalently alongside such racial categories as "Asian," "Black," and "non-Hispanic White" and tabulates data accordingly, the former have de facto become racial terms. Furthermore, the media and standardized tests and application forms of various types use the terms "Hispanic" and "Latino," reifying them as a racial category.

Before Directive 15, and dating back to 1850, the census category analogous to today's "Hispanic" was "Mexican origin." The U.S. census relied on several different indicators to identify persons of Mexican origin in those early decennial counts, such as country of birth (or parent's birth) and mother tongue. A century later, in the 1950s, the Census Bureau used Spanish surname to identify people of Mexican origin in five southwestern states, and first published information on persons of Puerto Rican birth or parentage who resided on the mainland. High rates of intermarriage and geographic mobility gradually undermined the usefulness of Spanish surname and language for enumerating Mexicans and Puerto Ricans. So, too, did the large numbers of Filipino immigrants, whose Spanish surnames hampered application of the Census Bureau's algorithm for identifying persons of Mexican ancestry living in the southwest. The changing composition of expanding migration flows from Latin America also warranted a more inclusive identifier that could accommodate all Spanish-speaking nationalities.

In the late 1960s, the U.S. Inter-Agency Committee on Mexican American Affairs, a federal task force established to ensure that Mexican Americans received a fair share of government services and programs, challenged the Census Bureau's plans for the 1970 census. The committee maintained that the traditional practice of relying on surnames, mother tongue, and birthplace produced a significant undercount of the population.[7] Not only did this vocal political constituency apply pressure on the Bureau to revise how it enumerated people of Hispanic origin, but more important, it triggered a systematic review of methods used to count all minority populations and to produce racial and ethnic statistics. Despite the Census Bureau's staunch objection to using subjective self-report questions to measure ethnicity, the 1970 census was the first to use a subjective identification question to enumerate the Spanish-origin—now Hispanic/Latino—population on the 5 percent sample questionnaire.

Of course, as suggested above, there is no archetypal Hispanic—not now and not in 1970. Many factors—intermarriage between Hispanics and non-Hispanics; generational variations; legal status; and often marked differences in levels of assimilation, educational attainment, and physical appearance—all contribute to a rather loose definition of the term "Hispanic." As noted, moreover, the criteria and labels used to classify people from Spanish-speaking America are themselves in flux—from "Spanish surname" and "Spanish heritage" to "Hispanic" and "Latino"—mirroring the many ways Hispanicity can be expressed in panethnic terms: as a distinctive racial identity, as an artifact of identity politics, and as a set of lived experiences. Moreover, the labels "Hispanic" and "Latino" are both celebrated (as in Hispanic Heritage Month) and stigmatized as a result of negative social connotations, especially those associated with legal status.

Whether the broad labels "Hispanic" and "Latino" ever acquire true panethnic status will depend largely on whether cross-cultural solidarity, mutual interests, and political cohesion materialize. It is ironic that one presumption of similarity—origin in a Spanish-speaking country—is now a key source of differentiation among Hispanic groups. As discussed in Chapter 2, larger numbers of new immigrants from Central and South America and the Dominican Republic are altering the U.S. Hispanic mosaic—still dominated by Mexicans but increasingly less so by Puerto Ricans and Cubans.

THE SHIFTING CONCEPT OF RACE

All U.S. censuses since 1790 have included questions about race; as the first decennial census to implement OMB Directive 15, however, the 1980 census short form asked all U.S. residents to indicate whether they were "of Spanish/Hispanic origin or descent."[8] In the 1980 and 1990 census questionnaires, the race question preceded the Hispanic origin item, which offered four main options:

- Mexican, Mexican American, Chicano
- Puerto Rican
- Cuban
- Other Spanish/Hispanic

Respondents selecting the last option were asked further to specify their "otherness," giving examples such as Argentinean, Colombian, Dominican, Nicaraguan, and Salvadoran. Census 2000 added the term "Latino" along-side "Spanish" and "Hispanic," but placed the Spanish/Hispanic/Latino item before the race question (see Figure 3-1).

Racial and ethnic classifications aim to reflect current social realities, but for Hispanics the Census Bureau's questions about race appeared to be curious at best. Not only did the 1980 census short form not use the word "race" to distinguish blacks, whites, Asians, and Native Americans (as stipulated by Directive 15), but as noted, the placement of the Hispanic origin and race questions differed from that used in 2000 (see Figure 3-1).[9] Race has a different meaning in Latin America, where Africans, indigenous peoples, and Europeans have long coexisted in large numbers.[10] For people of the Americas, whose concepts of race transcend the classic black–white divide, racial classification in the 1980 census (which included six Asian nationalities along with Samoan, Guamanian, and Hawaiian as separate "races") led to widespread confusion. A large number of Hispanics and others did not recognize the intended distinction between the racial and ethnic categories, including many newcomers unaccustomed to racial categories.

In 1980, more than one in three Hispanics self-identified as "some other race"; this figure was more than 40 percent in 1990.[11] As a result of political pressures to acknowledge the nation's increasing racial complexity and in an effort to adhere to OMB's directive that Hispanics could be of any race, census 2000 instructed respondents to answer both the "race" and "Hispanic origin" questions. It also permitted them to mark multiple race categories.[12] Unlike the 1980 and 1990 schedules, however, census 2000 provided no examples of Spanish-speaking nationalities, while continuing to list Asian nationalities as separate races. Not surprisingly, close to half of all Hispanics self-identified as "some other race" in census 2000. Dominicans (58 percent) were most likely to do so, while Cubans (7 percent) were least likely.[13] By contrast, only 3 percent of non-Hispanics classified themselves as "some other race."

The ethnic labels "Hispanic" and "Latino" are used so frequently along-side racial labels such as "Asian" and "black" that many Hispanics are beginning to view themselves as a separate race. Their choice of "some other race" on census forms reflects more than four centuries of *mestizaje*, or racial miscegenation, in Latin America and the Caribbean, as well as the differing conceptions of race noted above.[14] Hispanics may also mark "some

1970 Census

2. HOW IS EACH PERSON RELATED TO THE HEAD OF THIS HOUSEHOLD?	3. SEX	4. COLOR OR RACE
Fill one circle.	↯	↯
If "Other relative of head," also give exact relationship, for example, mother-in-law, brother, niece, grandson, etc.		*Fill one circle.*
If "Other not related to head," also give exact relationship, for example, partner, maid, etc.	Fill one circle	*If "Indian (American)," also give tribe.*
o Head of household　　o Roomer, boarder, lodger	Male	*If "Other," also give race.*
o Wife of head　　o Patient or inmate	o	o White　o Japanese　o Hawaiian
o Son or daughter of head　　o Other not related to head- *Print exact*		o Chinese　o Korean
o Other relative　　　　　　　*relationship*	Female	o Negro　o Filipino　o Other- *Print*
of head- *Print exact*	o	or Black　　　　　　　　*race*
relationship →　┈┈┈┈┈┈┈┈┈┈┈┈ ↙		Indian (Amer.) →┈┈┈┈┈┈┈ ↙
		Print Tribe

13a. Where was this person born? *If born in hospital, give State or country where mother lived. If born outside U.S., see instruction sheet: distinguish Northern Ireland from Ireland (Eire).*

　　o This State
　　OR
　　┈┈┈┈┈┈┈┈┈┈┈┈┈┈┈┈┈┈┈┈┈┈┈┈┈┈┈┈┈┈
　　(Name of state or foreign country; or Puerto Rico, Guam, etc.)

b. Is this person's origin or descent— *(Fill one circle)*

　　o Mexican　　　o Central or South American
　　o Puerto Rican　o Other Spanish
　　o Cuban　　　　o No, none of the above

14. What country was his father born in?
　　o United States
　　OR
　　┈┈┈┈┈┈┈┈┈┈┈┈┈┈┈┈┈┈┈┈┈┈┈┈┈┈┈┈┈┈
　　(Name of foreign country; or Puerto Rico, Guam, etc.)

1980 Census

Here are the QUESTIONS ↓	These are the columns for ANSWERS → *Please fill one column for each person listed in Question 1.*	PERSON in column 1		PERSON in column 2	
		Last name		Last name	
		First name　　　Middle initial		First name　　　Middle initial	
2. How is this person related to the person in column 1?				If relative of person in column 1:	
Fill one circle.		*START in this column with the household member (or one of the members) in whose name the home is owned or rented. If there is no such person, start in this column with any adult household member.*		o Husband/wife　o Father/mother	
				o Son/daughter　o Other relative ↙	
				o Brother/sister	
If "Other relative" of person in column 1, give exact relationship, such as mother-in-law, niece, grandson, etc.				If not related to person in column 1:	
				o Roomer/boarder　o Other nonrelative	
				o Partner/roommate ↙	
				o Paid employee	
3. Sex　*Fill one circle.*		o Male	o Female	o Male	o Female
4. Is this person –		o White	o Asian Indian	o White	o Asian Indian
		o Black or Negro	o Hawaiian	o Black or Negro	o Hawaiian
		o Japanese	o Guamanian	o Japanese	o Guamanian
		o Chinese	o Samoan	o Chinese	o Samoan
Fill one circle.		o Filipino	o Eskimo	o Filipino	o Eskimo
		o Korean	o Aleut	o Korean	o Aleut
		o Vietnamese	o Other – Specify ↙	o Vietnamese	o Other – Specify ↙
		o Indian (Amer.)		o Indian (Amer.)	
		Print tribe ┈┈┈┈		*Print tribe* ┈┈┈┈	

7. Is this person of Spanish/Hispanic origin or descent?	
Fill one circle.	o No (not Spanish/Hispanic)
	o Yes, Mexican, Mexican-Amer., Chicano
	o Yes, Puerto Rican
	o Yes, Cuban
	o Yes, other Spanish/Hispanic

FIGURE 3-1 1970, 1980, 1990, and 2000 census questionnaires: Race and Hispanic origin questions.

1990 Census

4. **Race** Fill ONE circle for the race that the person considers himself/herself to be. **If Indian (Amer.)**, print the name of the enrolled or principal tribe. **If Other Asian or Pacific Islander (API)**, print one group, for example, Hmong, Fijian, Laotian, Thai, Tongan, Pakistani, Cambodian, and so on. **If Other race**, print race.	o White o Black or Negro o Indian (Amer.) (Print the name of the enrolled or principal tribe) o Eskimo o Aleut Asian or Pacific Islander (API) o Chinese o Japanese o Filipino o Asian Indian o Hawaiian o Samoan o Korean o Guamanian o Vietnamese o Other API o Other race (Print race)	o White o Black or Negro o Indian (Amer.) (Print the name of the enrolled or principal tribe) o Eskimo o Aleut Asian or Pacific Islander (API) o Chinese o Japanese o Filipino o Asian Indian o Hawaiian o Samoan o Korean o Guamanian o Vietnamese o Other API o Other race (Print race)
7. **Is this person of Spanish/Hispanic origin?** FILL ONE circle for each person. **If Yes, other Spanish/Hispanic,** print one group.	o No (not Spanish/Hispanic) o Yes, Mexican, Mexican-Am., Chicano o Yes, Puerto Rican o Yes, Cuban o Yes, other Spanish/Hispanic (Print one group, for example: Argentinean, Colombian, Dominican, Nicaraguan, Salvadoran, Spaniard, and so on.)	o No (not Spanish/Hispanic) o Yes, Mexican, Mexican-Am., Chicano o Yes, Puerto Rican o Yes, Cuban o Yes, other Spanish/Hispanic (Print one group, for example: Argentinean, Colombian, Dominican, Nicaraguan, Salvadoran, Spaniard, and so on.)

2000 Census

5 Is this person Spanish/Hispanic/Latino? *Mark x the "No" box if **not** Spanish/Hispanic/Latino.*

☐ **No,** not Spanish/Hispanic/Latino
☐ Yes, Mexican, Mexican-Am., Chicano
☐ Yes, Puerto Rican
☐ Yes, Cuban
☐ Yes, other Spanish/Hispanic/Latino – *Print group.*

6 What is this person's race? Mark x one or more races to indicate what this person considers himself/herself to be.

☐ White
☐ Black, African Am., or Negro
☐ American Indian or Alaska Native – Print name of enrolled or principal tribe.

☐ Asian Indian   ☐ Native Hawaiian
☐ Chinese   ☐ Guamanian or Chamorro
☐ Filipino   ☐ Samoan
☐ Korean   ☐ Other Pacific Islander – *Print race.*
☐ Vietnamese
☐ Other Asian – *Print race.*

☐ Some other race – *Print race.*

other race" simply because they do not see themselves as fitting under any of the categories provided by the Census Bureau. In census 2000, Hispanics were more than three times as likely as non-Hispanics to claim an admixture of "two or more races," with most specifying "white" plus another race. Thus, their rejection of the OMB racial classification by checking "some other race" on the census questionnaire reflected their lived experience rather than a statistical artifact or measurement error.

The national differences among Hispanics discussed earlier add complexity to these racial contours. In the 2000 census, for example, four in five Cubans self-identified racially as white, but only one in five Dominicans did so; only 8 percent of Dominicans considered themselves black, as did less than 1 percent of Mexicans, Salvadorans, Guatemalans, Colombians, Peruvians, and Ecuadorians. Yet more than half of Dominicans, Salvadorans, and Guatemalans considered themselves "another race," as did roughly half of all Mexicans, Peruvians, Ecuadorians, and Puerto Ricans and just about a quarter of Colombians.

There are signs that the children of Latin American immigrants are even more likely than their parents to consider themselves "another race"— not black, white, Asian, or American Indian—which attests to a fluidity of racial identity that contrasts sharply with the historical black-white divide.[15] In the mid-1990s, more than 5,000 second-generation youths from south Florida and southern California representing 77 different nationalities, including all of the main Spanish-speaking countries of Latin America, were given the option to identify themselves racially as white, black, Asian, multiracial, or other.[16] More than three in four selected multiracial or other (the majority choosing other). Of those who chose other as their race, 41 percent indicated Hispanic or Latino, and another 20 percent cited their nationality (e.g., Mexican).[17]

In contrast, the children of Haitians, Jamaicans, and other West Indians tended to identify themselves racially as did their parents—most of whom self-identified as black. The same was true for Europeans and Canadians, the majority of whom labeled themselves white, and for Asian-origin youth, who generally identified as "Asian," as did their parents. Those of Latin American origin displayed by far the widest parent–child disparities in racial identity. Overall, about 60 percent of Latin American parents designated themselves as white, but only 20 percent of their own children did so. By nationality, the figures for parents versus children were 93 and 41 percent for Cubans; 85 and 24 percent for Colombians; approximately 67 and 20 percent for Salvadorans, Guatemalans, and Nicaraguans; and about 31 and 14 percent for Dominicans.

Hispanics' generational self-identity shift from white to multiracial is unprecedented. Among earlier immigrants, particularly those from southern and Eastern Europe, social acceptance and cultural assimilation often involved shifting racially from nonwhite to white. The generational shift among Hispanics reveals how, with time, the classification scheme proposed by Directive 15 has expanded the meaning of the labels "Hispanic" and "Latino," transforming them into ethnic identities that also have a racial component.

Children of immigrants exposed to American culture and its definitions of race during their formative years and later classified as Hispanic or Latino at school internalize the belief that they are members of a racial minority. They render their Hispanicity racial by expressing their national origin in those terms. This has far-reaching consequences for the contours of minority group boundaries and potentially, therefore, for intergroup relations. The situation illustrates the arbitrary nature of racial constructs—indeed, the ease with which an "ethnic" category developed for administrative purposes becomes a potent marker of social difference. It also implies that Hispanics are blurring former black-white racial boundaries, although the implications for the country's racial hierarchy are as yet unclear.[18]

Hispanicity, then, is both imagined and real: imagined because it is a social construct invented by the federal government for the purpose of bureaucratic accounting, and real because it has been rendered so by its use. Through their broad popular usage, the ethnoracial labels "Hispanic" and "Latino" are increasingly being accepted by immigrants and their U.S.-born children as referring to their own identities. The extent of the impact of these labels as markers of differences in status remains an open question, to be settled by the second and later generations.

ESPAÑOL OR ENGLISH?

English is the door to the American dream. Not until one masters el inglés are the fruits of that dream attainable.[19]

Unlike the European immigrants who crossed the Atlantic en masse from the 1880s to the 1920s and those from Asia who did so after legal barriers had been removed in the late 1960s, immigrants from Mexico, most of Central and South America, and the Spanish-speaking Caribbean speak a common language: Spanish. This fact—not place, not race, not citizenship—is the single greatest difference between Hispanics and non-Hispanics in the United States. As a core issue in the Hispanic experience, language raises important questions about divided national loyalties and the cohesion of Hispanicity as a panethnic identity; about social integration and labor market prospects in an English-dominant society; and, more generally, about the terms of belonging in U.S. society. In this context, and independent from discussions of educational policy, bilingualism is an essential dimension of language shift with major implications for social integration.[20]

Altogether, more than 28 million U.S. residents ages 5 and older spoke Spanish at home in 2000—about 10 million more than the total number of persons who spoke all other languages combined. To a casual observer, particularly in areas where Hispanics are highly concentrated, the ubiquity of Spanish—on storefronts, on election ballots, and in airports, for example—signals the emergence of a bilingual nation by default, if not by design. Although this may be the case on the streets of America, in fact the pervasiveness of Spanish-language use at home is a transitory phenomenon that largely reflects immigration patterns. It is true that the vast majority of Hispanics born abroad—93 percent—speak some Spanish at home, compared with only 63 percent of those native born. What those figures fail to convey, however, is that among remaining bilinguals Spanish fluency erodes rapidly over time and across generations.

Unlike foreign-born young people, who have an opportunity to improve their linguistic skills as they progress through U.S. schools, relatively few adults who immigrate pursue their education beyond age 25. This reduces the labor market prospects of foreign-born, working-age Hispanics compared with whites or blacks, who are largely proficient in English. Only one-third of foreign-born working-age Hispanics are fluent in English, compared with about 88 percent of their U.S.-born counterparts and virtually all non-Hispanic blacks and whites. Men and women are about equally proficient in English, but notable differences occur across Hispanic subgroups. Roughly a quarter of Mexican immigrants claim fluency in English, compared with half of Cubans born abroad and even larger shares of island-born Puerto Ricans. These differences reflect mainly length of U.S. residence and to a lesser extent educational levels. Variation in English fluency is minimal among U.S.-born Hispanics, with proficiency levels hovering around 90 percent for the three largest subgroups—Mexicans, Puerto Ricans, and Cubans (see Figure 3-2).

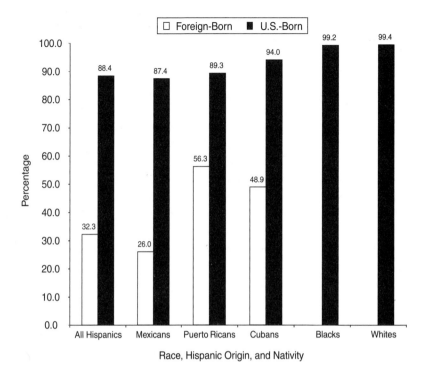

FIGURE 3-2 Percentage of working-age adults who speak English very well by race, Hispanic origin, and nativity.
NOTE: The samples include individuals ages 25 to 59. In these tabulations, persons who speak only English are presumed to speak English "very well."
SOURCE: 2000 census, 5 percent samples, Public Use Microdata Samples (PUMS).

The degree of Spanish retention among foreign-born Hispanics remains a subject of considerable controversy because of the presumption that bilingualism retards the acquisition of English-language skills. The loyalty that many Spanish speakers (especially Mexicans) feel toward their native tongue diminishes across generations, especially beyond the second. A recent national survey of Hispanic immigrants revealed that 72 percent were Spanish dominant, 25 percent were bilingual, and a mere 4 percent were English dominant. By the second generation, only 7 percent of adult Hispanics were Spanish dominant, and about 47 percent each were bilingual or English dominant. Among the third and later generations, not only did Spanish dominance disappear, but fewer than one-quarter were bilingual.[21] Similarly, a rare multigenerational study of Mexican-origin couples in Los Angeles conducted in the mid-1970s found that among first-generation (immigrant) women, 84 percent used only Spanish at home, 14 percent used both languages, and a mere 2 percent used only English. By the third generation, there was a complete reversal of these shares, with 4 percent speaking only Spanish at home, 12 percent using both languages, and 84 percent speaking only English.[22]

Of the three main factors that shape English fluency among the foreign born—length of time in the United States, age at arrival in the United States, and educational attainment—the latter two are the most decisive. The younger the immigrant at the time of arrival and the more educated, the greater is the facility in acquiring English-language skills.[23] For working-age adults, particularly those with low levels of completed schooling, the propensity to learn English is much lower, sometimes for lack of access to a supportive language program. Nevertheless, there are strong indications that Hispanics are shifting from Spanish to English at an increasingly rapid pace. The most compelling evidence is from data that record changes in language preferences over time. The Children of Immigrants Longitudinal Study (CILS), which collected data over a 10-year period for first- and second-generation Hispanic youths as they made their transition to adulthood, showed rapid linguistic assimilation, even among the groups most likely to retain Spanish: Mexicans living along the U.S.-Mexican border and Cubans residing in Miami, the most bilingual major city in the country.[24]

In focus group sessions commissioned by the panel and conducted over several months, participants emphasized repeatedly how they wanted their children to be able to speak Spanish, even if they themselves lacked facility with the language. Third-generation Hispanics, in particular, stressed the importance of repairing the breaks in the cultural chain that occurred when their own parents failed to keep the Spanish language alive at home. The following comments made to the panel were typical:

> You don't need to speak Spanish to be considered a "white-washed Hispanic," or at least I am, because I don't speak Spanish. What I speak, I learned in school, and I don't speak it well. My parents are fluent. I'm white-washed because I'm losing the culture. (third-generation Hispanic, Houston)
>
> My mom made the decision not to teach me Spanish because she wanted me to learn English well. Now my Dad's mad at her because I don't speak any Spanish. I think they spoke Spanish amongst each other when they didn't

want me to know what they were talking about. Being around it, you learn. I don't speak it but I understand it. So, they know better. (third-generation Hispanic, Houston)

"Spanglish"—a creative if jumbled blending of Spanish and English spoken widely among U.S. Hispanics both at home and abroad—may be an important part of the process by which Hispanicity is forged in the context of cultural shift (see the example in Box 3-1). Widely regarded as the tongue of the uneducated, Spanglish is the quintessential hybrid—"the verbal encounter between Anglo and Hispano civilizations."[25] It is spoken testimony to attempted communication between immigrant populations and mainstream America that preserves as much of the native tongue as is practicable. According to Stavans, "This delicious—and delirious—mish-mash is what Latino identity is about: the verbal mestizaje that results from a transient people, *un pueblo en movimiento.*"[26] The evolution of the language itself is a powerful symbol of hybrid identities that cut across national, racial, and social boundaries.

BOX 3-1
Example of Spanglish

They want me pa'las quotas, so the place might say "chicanos are also part of our diverse population." Pero pa'que, profe? I don't feel bien. I'm just a strange animal brought in a cage to be displayed pa'que los gringos no sientan culpa.[27]

In sum, rapid linguistic assimilation among youths from all Hispanic subgroups and social classes points to a clear and inevitable decline in their use of, preference for, and therefore fluency in Spanish. Hence like other immigrant groups, the majority of third-generation Hispanics—the grand-children of the present wave of immigrants—will be English monolinguals. The only prominent exceptions to this trend are Dominicans, who main-tain very close contact with their homeland.[28]

Despite the high level of immigration during the 1980s and 1990s, the shift to English may actually be occurring at a more accelerated rate today than was true in the past. The experience of Mexican youths is most telling on this point: in 1990, already about two-thirds of third-generation children spoke only English at home; a decade later, the equivalent figure was about 71 percent.[29] Arguably, the atrophy of these children's ability to maintain fluency in the language of their immigrant grandparents represents a significant loss of valuable bilingual resources, both for individuals and for the United States in a global economy. Increased awareness of the value of this linguistic and cultural resource could retard the process of language loss by promoting bilingualism with strong English proficiency, but not without explicit recognition that proficiency in two languages is an asset.[30] Whether this opportunity will be seized is uncertain, but current trends are not encouraging.

CONCLUSION

How immigrant and minority groups self identify—and are identified—is a gauge of their integration in U.S. society. Hispanicity as an identity has its roots in U.S. laws and regulations, embodied in questions included on the U.S. census since 1970 on the long form and since 1980 on the short form. The term "Hispanic," however, is deceptive because it masks the great diversity among the Hispanic population and implies a monolithic group that does not exist. Whether it evolves into an enduring panethnic identity will partly depend on whether social and political cohesion evolves among Hispanic subgroups. A better understanding of Hispanics' intergenerational change awaits the inclusion of questions on parental birthplace in the U.S. census and other major data sources with sufficiently large samples (see Box 3-2).

For the government's purposes, Hispanic is considered an ethnic identity ("Hispanics may be of any race"). But socially, and in popular use, there are signs that Hispanic connotes both an ethnic and a racial identity, particularly among second and later generation Hispanics.

Whether "Hispanic" will evolve to become a symbolic identity or whether it will be an enduring marker of ethnic and minority group status is highly uncertain. If Hispanics successfully integrate into the societal mainstream, as earlier immigrant groups have done, then the former is likely to be true. Language trends suggest that this integration is taking place. But other crucial indicators of social integration are less clear. The next chapter continues the examination of integration, turning to the social, economic, and political contexts in which it is taking place.

BOX 3-2
The Need for Improved Data

Before 1970 knowledge about the Hispanic population was largely regional in scope because of the Census Bureau's reliance on objective indicators, such as Spanish surname, birthplace, parents' birthplace, and mother tongue to identify people of Spanish ancestry or descent. The Spanish origin item, first introduced in the 1969 Current Population Survey (CPS) on an experimental basis and then included in the 5 percent schedule of the 1970 census, allowed for the enumeration of the Hispanic population on a national basis. Although the 1980 census improved the Hispanic enumeration by including the Spanish origin item on the 100 percent schedule, the replacement of the parents' birthplace item, which was used to represent generational status from 1870 to 1970, with a question about ancestry compromised the ability to portray intergenerational changes. Consequently, the measurement of Hispanics' intergenerational progress has been limited to surveys with detailed information about generational status.

There is a pressing need for additional data on parental birthplace to provide information about the generational status of Hispanics (and other groups) and enable the tracking of intergenerational mobility. Neither the census, which is the primary source for information on the foreign born in the United States, nor the American Community Survey (ACS), intended to replace the census long form, asks this question.[31]

The annual CPS, conducted by the Census Bureau for the Bureau of Labor Statistics, does include questions about parental nativity. The responses to these questions yield valuable information for the study of immigrants and their children.

However, the CPS is based on a sample rather than a full enumeration—hence it generates "estimates" rather than enumerated generational composition. The CPS is also hampered by small sample sizes. When the available data are broken down by national origin and generational cohort, cell sizes do not permit reliable analyses, even if multiple years of the survey are merged.[32] In the CPS, "third generation" includes a substantial share of persons of fourth, fifth, and higher-order generational status.

These problems can be remedied by adding questions about parental nativity to the census and the ACS and other major data sources. There is also a need for samples that are large enough to enable the study of national-origin groups by generation, with appropriate controls on salient variables. Having Spanish-language versions of survey instruments will avoid the exclusion of participation on the basis of language.

NOTES

1 A JSTOR search identified early use of Hispanic in the social science literature in the late 1930s, mainly referring to geography, with a major increase in use in the mid-1970s, which coincided with the official use to designate people of Spanish or Latin American origin. Latinos used in a classical sense dates back to the 18th century. It began to be used widely to refer to Latin American populations in the 1960s.

2 The term "Spanish origin," which was used in 1970, could be used in addition to Hispanic or Latino.

3 See Castillo, 2003; Fears, 2003; Portes and Rumbaut, 2001; and Sachs, 2001. The term "Hispanic" at least invites an association with the Spanish language, which "Latino" cannot. For recent national evidence on adults' preferences for the two panethnic labels, see Pew Hispanic Center/Kaiser Family Foundation, 2002.

4 Sachs, 2001:1.

5 Choldin, 1986.

6 In response to political pressure in 1997, the terminology was officially modified to "Hispanic/Latino" and "not of Hispanic/Latino" origin.

7 The Census Bureau's analysis of traditional identifiers, such as surname, using the results of Hispanic self-identification in the 1973 Current Population Survey, confirmed the undercount charges levied by the Inter-Agency Committee on Mexican American Affairs. Choldin, 1986:410, reports that in the Southwest, where the Spanish surname item was used, only 81 percent of those with Spanish surnames identified themselves as Hispanic, and only 74 percent of those who self-identified as Hispanic had Spanish surnames. However, results for the rest of the nation were even more problematic, as only 46 percent of persons with Spanish surnames self-identified as Hispanic, while 61 percent of persons who self-identified as Hispanic had Spanish surnames.

8 Technically, the 1970 census was the first to use a subjective Spanish origin identifier on a national basis, but the questionable wording, the number of response categories, the placement of the non-Spanish response, and the population coverage (asked of only 5 percent of households) yielded highly problematic results. See Bean and Tienda, 1987: Chapter 2.

9 See Bean and Tienda, 1987:Chapter 2; Choldin, 1986.

10 Race is clearly an important sorting mechanism throughout Latin America, producing a racial hierarchy, but in general race is not associated with the deep schisms found in mainstream U.S. society. See Telles, 2004.

11 Haney López, 2004.

12 Census dress rehearsals revealed that many non-Hispanics did not answer the Hispanic question when it was asked after the race question. This decision also was motivated by a desire to reduce nonresponse among whites.

13 Tafoya, 2004:6.

14 Telles, 2004.

15 Lee and Bean, 2004.

16 Portes and Rumbaut, 2001.

17 Portes and Rumbaut, 2001:Table 7-7.

18 Lee and Bean, 2004.

19 Stavans, 2003:3.

20 López, 1996; Portes and Rumbaut, 2001.

21 Pew Hispanic Center, Assimilation and Language, 2004:Table 2.

22 López, 1978. Among the men, the pattern was similar except that their shift to English by the second generation was even more marked.

23 Rumbaut, 2006:Table 10.

24 The CILS is described in Portes and Rumbaut, 2001.

25 Stavans, 2003:5.

26 Stavans, 2003:35.

27 Stavans, 2003:35.

28 Alba, 2004.

29 Alba, 2004; Alba et al., 2002.

30 Pew Hispanic Center, Assimilation and Language, 2004.

31 The American Community Survey asks the same questions about migration and foreign birth that were asked in census 2000, including place of birth of the respondent, citizenship status, year of entry, ancestry, and language spoken at home—but not parental birthplace.

32 Rumbaut, 2004.

Patssi Valdez

Sunflowers with Purple Heart (2002)

Copyright by the artist; used with permission.

4

The Challenges of Integration

Hispanics' social, economic, and political well-being depends crucially on opportunities to earn a living, to contribute to and share in national prosperity, and to become empowered socially and politically. In short, the integration pathways of newcomers, the economic prospects of the emerging second generation, and the social mobility of established residents together will shape the future of Hispanics in the United States. While in some respects the Hispanic experience mirrors that of other immigrant groups, there are important differences between the economic and demographic profile of the United States now and a century ago, when previous immigration flows reached their historical peak. In particular, three significant conditions existing today in the United States will color the Hispanic experience in the decades to come: the changing social contract, evolving economic trends, and the aging of the white majority. In addition, the historical tendency for Hispanic immigrants to cluster regionally and in urban ethnic neighborhoods has changed; Hispanics today are transforming the face of American cities and towns as they disperse to new destinations across the nation. Accompanying these new trends is the evolution of Hispanic voices in the nation's political arenas.

THE CHANGING SOCIAL CONTRACT

America's social contract has become more conservative over the last 25 years. As a result, safety nets that protect children and families have become less dependable, and social policies have sharpened distinctions between immigrants and citizens and between the young and the old. The Personal Responsibility and Work Opportunity Reconciliation Act, a sweeping welfare reform bill signed into law by President Clinton in 1996, signaled a dramatic shift in U.S. income security policy for immigrants and the poor. Replacing the long-standing Aid to Families with Dependent Children program with Temporary Assistance to Needy Families, the new legislation imposed time limits on cash assistance benefits and required adults to work or participate in education or training programs in exchange for benefits.

Policy changes in the education and health domains also have far-reaching implications for the future welfare of Hispanics of all ages. Skyrocketing health insurance premiums have forced many two-parent working families to drop their health care coverage and also have taken a significant toll on small businesses, which have had to scale back benefits, increase copayments and employee contributions, or cease offering insurance plans altogether. In the last 3 years alone, businesses with fewer than 99 employees have witnessed a decline in health care coverage from 57 to 50 percent.[1] This trend is particularly detrimental to Hispanics, who are more highly concentrated in small firms than are non-Hispanics. In 1997, for example, nearly half of Hispanic nonagricultural workers were employed in firms with 99 or fewer employees, compared with 43 percent of non-Hispanics.[2]

In the realm of higher education, waning federal support for low-income students to attend college has coincided with above-average tuition hikes designed to offset shortfalls in state and local budgets—just when growing numbers of students, an increasing number of them Hispanic, have been requesting financial aid. When the Pell program was created, for example, the maximum grant covered 84 percent of college expenses for the neediest students; today it covers just one-third of those expenses. (The subject of education is discussed in detail in Chapter 5.)

ECONOMIC TRENDS

The United States features the most inequitable distribution of wealth and income among industrialized nations. Not since the Jazz Age of the 1920s has the imbalance in income and wealth been greater. Currently, the top 1 percent of all households enjoy more pretax income than the bottom 40 percent.[3] Wealth inequalities are even more pronounced. The rise in wage inequality has been traced to technological change, which requires higher labor market skills and gives more-educated workers wage premiums. It has also been linked to a decline in unionization and to a minimum wage infrequently adjusted for inflation.[4] There is some evidence that immigration may have contributed to the increase in economic inequality in the United States by depressing the earnings of the lowest skilled workers.[5]

Inequality in U.S. wages began to climb about three decades ago, coinciding with the surge in Hispanic immigration. The steady rise in inflation-adjusted wages that began after World War II ended during the early 1970s, when a decade of high inflation was followed by a decade of high unemployment. Both periods were accompanied by the decline of durable manufacturing industries and the expansion of service industries. Although real wages grew a brisk 8.3 percent between 1995 and 2001 after a prolonged stagnation, earnings inequality rose yet again.[6] The top 20 percent of male workers earned about 6 times as much as the bottom 20 percent in 1973, as compared with 10 times as much in 2001.[7]

Young workers with only a high school education or less—precisely the demographic profile characterizing recent Hispanic immigrants (see Chapter 5)—were hardest hit by the wage erosion that began in the early 1970s.[8] Compared with the postwar period through 1973, workers lacking a college education today have a more difficult time making ends meet. Between 1973 and 1996, the average real wage of male high school graduates fell almost $3.00 per hour—$4.00 for those without a diploma. Despite the robust economy of the late 1990s, which allowed low-skill groups to recoup some of these wage declines, their 2001 hourly wages remained below those earned by their low-skilled counterparts in 1973. By contrast, real wages of male college graduates were unchanged between 1973 and 1996, but rose during the late 1990s.[9]

As a result of these trends job growth is now greatest for higher-skilled occupations, with more moderate expansion in low-end, low-wage service sector jobs. Meanwhile, midlevel occupations have declined; specifically, between 1969 and 1999 there was growth at both ends of the occupational spectrum, while the middle slumped.[10] Service, sales, technical, professional, and managerial occupations each grew between 2 and 4 percentage points, while blue collar and support occupations declined precipitously—from 56 to 39 percent of all adult workers (see Figure 4-1).

The reduction in demand for less skilled workers and precarious economic prospects in today's economy have set the stage for both the risks and opportunities confronting the rapidly growing Hispanic population,

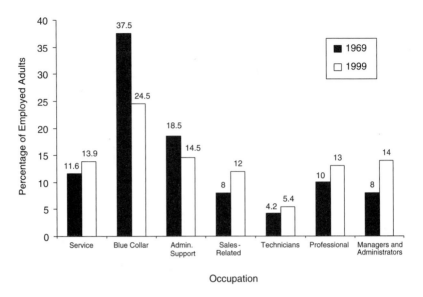

FIGURE 4-1 Adult occupational distribution: 1969 and 1999.
SOURCE: Figure 3-2 in Levy and Murnane (2004).

with its youthful age structure and low skill levels.[11] Young, unskilled workers are especially vulnerable to business cycle fluctuations and future changes in labor market demand. Better education is the single resource that in the long run will improve the economic prospects and social integration of the burgeoning Hispanic population. Despite significant improvements in high school and college graduation rates among young Hispanics since 1980, large education gaps remain in comparison with other groups, especially for Hispanic immigrants, but the prospects of the second generation are worrisome as well (see Chapter 5).

COMING OF AGE IN AN AGING SOCIETY

Not only are Hispanics forging their national presence in an age of rising inequality, but they are also coming of age in an aging society. Although the Hispanic population will continue to grow through immigration, it is primarily the U.S.-born children and grandchildren of immigrants—the rising second generation and their offspring—who will define its economic and social contours (see Chapter 2).[12] In 2000, children of Hispanic immigrants had a median age of just over 12 years. Thus, the impact of the youthful age structure and above-average birthrates of Hispanics is already being felt in schools today; it will be felt tomorrow in higher education and in labor markets.

With the exception of Mexicans and Puerto Ricans, most Hispanics are first-generation immigrants, but even 42 percent of Mexicans are foreign born. In 1960, a mere 5 percent of the U.S. population was foreign born, and only about 25 percent of Hispanics were born abroad or in Puerto Rico.[13] At the time, almost half of all Hispanics—primarily Mexicans—were U.S. born to U.S.-born parents. Just over one in four Hispanics (28 percent) were second generation. After four decades of immigration, the foreign-born share of the total U.S. population doubled to 11 percent, but the foreign-born share of Hispanics (exclusive of island-born Puerto Ricans) nearly tripled—from 14 to 40 percent. By 2030, the second generation is projected to represent 30 percent of the entire Hispanic population, and a third generation will be well on its way, thus sustaining the youthful composition of the Hispanic population (see Figure 4-2).

This infusion of young people into the United States is a potentially positive development, slowing the nation's overall population aging while partially offsetting the rising burden of dependency of an aging majority—what might be viewed as a demographic dividend. In 1960, less than 10 percent of the total U.S. population was of retirement age or older, compared with less than 3 percent of the Hispanic population. Four decades later, these proportions were more than 12 percent and less than 5 percent, respectively. This relative age difference is echoed in median ages of 39 and 27 years, respectively. A generation from now—by 2030—about 25 percent of white Americans will have reached retirement age or beyond, compared with only 10 percent of Hispanics, just when the burgeoning Hispanic second generation, with a median age of 21, will have reached its prime working years. But labor market impacts will occur well before this time as a result of Hispanics' younger average age at first employment and growing share of the working-age population (see Figure 4-3).

An aging industrialized society can balance its rising old-age dependency ratio by importing workers and raising women's labor force participation rates. In the absence of substantial productivity increases, however, such demographic solutions will be insufficient.[14] In particular, funding the pensions of a swelling elderly population requires a productive workforce capable of paying taxes, saving, and investing. Hispanic workers—immigrant and natives alike—already contribute to the social security system. In fact, illegal workers, the majority of whom are Hispanic,

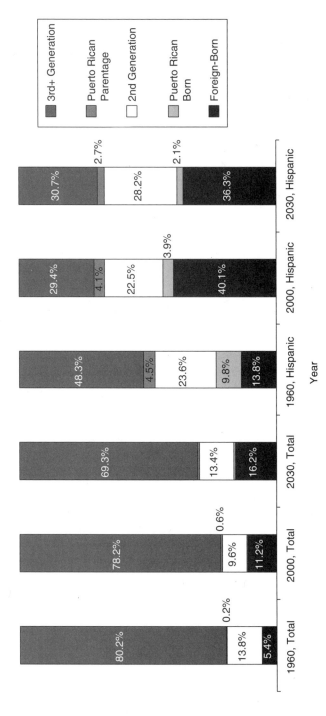

FIGURE 4-2 Generational transition of Hispanic and U.S. population: 1960, 2000, and 2030.
SOURCE: Passel (2004).

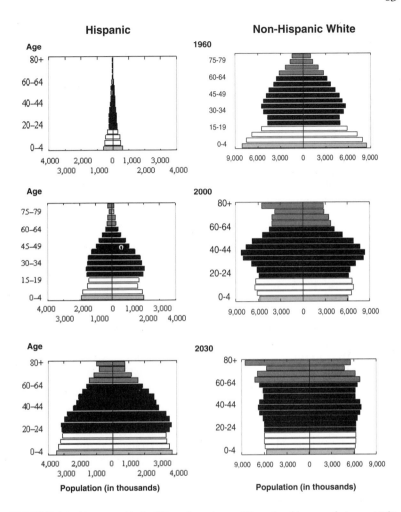

FIGURE 4-3 Age pyramids for Hispanic and non-Hispanic white populations: 1960, 2000, and projected 2030.
SOURCE: Passel (2004).

are estimated to contribute as much as $7 billion a year to social security without being entitled to any of the benefits.[15] Thus, immigrant labor can help to support the costs of an aging population, but their potential contributions depend on earnings capacity, which in turn depends on educational investments.

The potential dividend offered by working-age Hispanic immigrants and their future offspring is tempered by their relatively low average earning capacity on arrival. Given the very substantial differences in earnings, education, English fluency, attitudes, and median age between foreign-born and native-born Hispanics, the economic and social repercussions of the generational transformation now under way will depend largely on social investments in U.S.-born Hispanics—the second and later generations—with the proviso that this upward mobility might increase competition with currently more educated segments of the labor force. Hence the amount of Hispanic upward mobility that can be expected from future educational investments may be uncertain, but a sustained presence in low-wage jobs in the absence of significant educational improvement is a virtual certainty.

HISPANIC DISPERSAL

Until recently, the U.S. Hispanic population was concentrated regionally in the southwest, primarily near the southern border with Mexico; in the northeast, most notably in the greater New York and Boston metropolitan areas; and after 1960, in southern Florida. California and Texas have served as both ports of entry and final destinations for Mexican immigrants, and since 1980, for El Salvadorians and Guatemalans. Central and South American immigrants have settled largely in Florida—where they have diluted the Cuban ethnic hegemony—and in New York and New Jersey. In 2000, 7 of every 10 Hispanics resided in these five states. Other important immigrant-receiving states include Arizona, New Mexico, and Illinois—where Mexican neighborhoods emerged in the 1920s, and Puerto Rican communities flourished after World War II.

While these states continue to attract and retain the bulk of new arrivals, many Hispanic immigrants are now choosing to settle in non-traditional destinations such as the cities of the deep south. Significant Hispanic settlement is also occurring in rural areas of the south and midwest.[16] In fact, the state with the fastest-growing Hispanic population in the country is not California, nor is it Texas, Florida, Illinois, or New York; it is North Carolina. According to the Census Bureau, the Hispanic population in North Carolina grew five-fold during the 1990s—from 77,000 to 379,000, while that in Georgia quadrupled, and that in Nevada tripled.

In addition, areas once considered "capital cities" for immigrants from just one or two countries are witnessing ethnic diversification as various Hispanic subgroups vie for economic and social space. New York City, long the "home away from home" for Puerto Ricans, is now the principal destination for Dominicans, Ecuadorians, Panamanians, and Paraguayans. Mexicans are New York's fourth-largest Latin American group, while in Florida, Central Americans, Colombians, and Puerto Ricans collectively now outnumber Cubans, who remain politically dominant nonetheless.

Another distinctive feature of the Hispanic dispersal is that, in many cases, entire families are relocating rather than sending male workers on seasonal labor sojourns. Given the number of people and places involved, the geographic dispersal of Hispanics not only is redrawing spatial contours, but also may be reshaping the social and economic experiences of the Hispanics who settle in the new destinations.

Paradoxes of Place

The spatial dispersal of Hispanics presents an interesting paradox. Even as Hispanics are experiencing less regional segregation, they are finding themselves resegregated in both traditional settlement cities and their new destinations. By one account, between 1990 and 2000 Hispanic segregation from whites rose in 124 of 210 metropolitan areas, while it fell in 86—a net increase of 38 areas in which segregation increased. During this same period, black–white segregation declined in 240 of 265 metropolitan areas and remained stable in the remainder.[17] Whether and to what extent Hispanic geographic dispersal may have contributed to the decline in black–white segregation is unclear, but some experts claim that Hispanics are softening color lines because they are more likely than whites to share social space with blacks and Asians.[18]

Hispanics are generally less segregated in neighborhoods outside their traditional settlement areas, although levels of segregation vary greatly in the new destinations. Immigrants are typically more segregated residentially than their native-born counterparts, but this trend is highly variable and depends to some extent on the state of the economy.[19] In fact, the great diversity in levels of Hispanic residential segregation across metropolitan areas defies generalization. Multiethnic metropolitan areas with large and well-established Hispanic barrios, such as Los Angeles, Chicago, and San Francisco, are characterized by moderate overall segregation levels, relatively low exposure of Hispanics to blacks and Asians, and only moderate exposure to whites. Compared with the native born, Hispanics born abroad experience higher levels of social isolation, particularly in metropolitan areas such as Austin, Dallas, and Houston in Texas or Sacramento and San Diego in California, where immigration has fueled unusually rapid population growth.

The tendency for foreign-born Hispanics to cluster in high-density immigrant neighborhoods while they familiarize themselves with U.S. institutions and acquire proficiency in English largely explains their higher levels of social isolation. In 2000, Hispanic immigrants typically resided in neighborhoods where more than one-third of their neighbors were also foreign born and where fewer than half of their neighbors spoke English at home.[20] Although the residential concentration of newcomers with limited English proficiency may retard their cultural assimilation, their economic integration is not necessarily hampered because many new arrivals use their social ties with established Hispanic residents to find housing and work. To what extent preexisting social ties promote the integration of Hispanic immigrants in new destinations is not yet known, but the pace at which Hispanic communities are expanding in some of the new locations suggests that social networks both reinforce growth and facilitate settlement.

Engines of Growth

One factor driving the geographic dispersal of Hispanics is the lure of employment opportunities in rapidly growing, labor-intensive industries. Having gained a reputation as hard workers in southwestern and midwestern agricultural labor markets, Mexican immigrants have made their way to the agricultural belt between Florida and New Jersey, moving from south to north and back again in response to harvest seasons and putting down roots in areas that offer more-permanent work. The relocation of meat and poultry processing plants from cities to nonmetropolitan areas to reduce labor costs has opened up many opportunities for unskilled workers, often leaving thousands of unionized workers jobless as a result. The poultry and meat processing industries in Iowa, Minnesota, and Nebraska and the seafood industry along the East Coast have attracted numerous immigrants seeking stable employment, including many undocumented workers.[21]

In the new Hispanic destinations—primarily urban and suburban communities—there is expanding labor demand in construction, dwelling maintenance and repair services, private household services, and nondurable manufacturing. These industries are readily absorbing immigrant laborers searching for stable jobs in smaller, more affordable communities. In Nevada, for example, the Hispanic population swelled in response to a new phase of hotel and casino development that revived the construction industry. Now, Mexican immigrants dominate Nevada's hotel, casino, and restaurant service industries—jobs once held by blacks and poor white workers.[22] Nevada offered other advantages to migrants, such as affordable housing and lower living costs, permitting entire families to move and making Las Vegas and Reno more appealing than expensive gateway cities such as New York and Los Angeles, where the limited options of the barrios and long commutes to suburban jobs undermine family life.

Of the largest 100 U.S. metropolitan areas, 50 have been designated as "new Hispanic destinations." In those areas, Hispanics made up less than 2 percent of both the population and the workforce in 1980; by 2000, they represented 7 percent of the population in these areas and 7 percent of the labor force.[23] Hispanic job market niches in the new destinations mirror those in the more established Hispanic metropolitan destinations. Nonetheless, a noteworthy labor market transformation is occurring. The growing demand in these industries is being met by foreign-born rather than U.S.-born Hispanics (who presumably would have a stronger command of English). Some striking examples dramatize this point. While the occupational share of native-born Hispanics working as dwelling maintenance workers in the new destination areas inched up from 2 to 3 percent between 1980 and 2000, the share of foreign-born Hispanics in the same industry skyrocketed from less than 1 percent to 18 percent. The construction and private household industries in the new destination areas witnessed a similar evolution in the composition of their workforce after 1980.[24] From 1980 to 2000, the proportion of native-born Hispanics among all construction workers in the new destination labor markets rose from 1 to 2 percent, while that of foreign-born Hispanics rose from under 1 percent to over 10 percent. In the traditional metro areas, where immigration played a major role in population growth during the 1990s, similar trends are evident in the dwelling maintenance, construction, and domestic household work industries.

Uncertain Promises

The significance of rising Hispanic residential segregation in both traditional and new destinations is unclear. If the phenomenon is transitory and related to the tendency of immigrants to huddle in ethnic neighborhoods until they become familiar with U.S. institutions, spatial divisions should diminish over time as successive generations come of age. On the other hand, because spatial assimilation unfolds very gradually and is often accompanied by class and racial divisions, persistent spatial segregation could undermine Hispanics' long-term social integration. Much will depend on how well newcomers are received in the nontraditional locales; while immigrants are welcomed as hard workers in some communities, in others they increasingly experience a backlash of discrimination.[25]

Given that Hispanic geographic dispersal is a relatively recent occurrence, it is difficult to say which circumstances will promote integration and what divisions—ethnic, class, or language—will persist over the long run. The pace of assimilation for Hispanics arriving in the newer destinations will depend on, among other factors, the relative and absolute size of the black and Asian populations in the same communities, the proportion of recent immigrants in the overall population mix, and the size of the receiving community.

Two factors related to Hispanics' geographic dispersal have particularly important implications for their long-term prosperity—educational outcomes and home ownership rates. Hispanic dropout rates are disturbingly high in some of the new settlement areas.[26] In new destinations such as the south where Hispanic workers are typically illegal, have little education, and speak limited English, the educational challenges for their children are profound but not unsurmountable.[27]

To the extent that dispersal shifts Hispanics from high- to low-cost areas, home ownership rates should increase; however, the change will be gradual because lower-income immigrants, who are driving the geographic dispersal, are less likely than natives to own their homes.[28] Nevertheless, Hispanic home ownership rates have risen appreciably since 1980—from about 33 percent in 1983 to 44 percent in 2001—even as the share of immigrant Hispanic households has risen appreciably.[29] By one estimate, the home ownership rates of Hispanic immigrants approach those of native-born Hispanics after 20 years of U.S. residence.[30] This, too, may change, however, depending on whether and how integration unfolds in the new destinations. If limited access to affordable housing relegates Hispanic youths—the second generation in particular—to segregated, resource-poor schools, the benefits of home ownership among the current generation may well be offset by the diminished life options of future generations.

POLITICAL VOICE

Increased mass migration from Latin America and the Caribbean has generated a growing need to incorporate Hispanic voices into community and national politics. In addressing this need, it is important to recognize that popular but oversimplified references to "the" Hispanic political community or "the" Hispanic vote ignore the population's enormous diversity and ambivalence about panethnic identity (see Chapter 3). Over the last 20 years, Hispanic elites, particularly those of non-Cuban origin, have organized primarily under a panethnic umbrella rather than according to national-origin identities. The agendas of national organizations such as the Mexican American Legal Defense and Education Fund, the National Council of La Raza, and the Congressional Hispanic Caucus, while reflecting the considerable diversity of the Hispanic population, cross-cut nationalities and party affiliations. These national organizations have their local and regional Hispanic counterparts in areas of Latino concentration throughout the nation.

Despite their substantial class and status differences, Hispanic ethnic groups share a surprising number of social priorities. As a group Hispanics tend to support political positions associated with both conservative and liberal agendas—a characteristic that distinguishes them from typical political constituencies. Although seemingly contradictory, Hispanics' opposition to such practices as same-sex unions and abortion and their support for civil rights, higher taxation, and government-provided social benefits are both consistent with views that value collective over individual goals.[31] Yet Hispanics' weak political infrastructure at the national level undermines their opportunities for political cohesion even when such a disposition exists.[32]

Driving Hispanics' social policy agenda are the growing numbers— U.S.- and foreign-born alike—who recognize that their own and their children's socioeconomic progress depends on both civil rights protections and publicly funded social services, particularly education. Virtually all public opinion polls reveal that Hispanics consider education the single most important issue facing the nation, and themselves in particular. (As the subgroup with the oldest age structure, Cubans are somewhat more likely than other Hispanic subgroups to identify elderly assistance as a priority issue.)

The political agenda of Hispanics has a distinct social focus that distinguishes it from that of non-Hispanics, which is more likely to emphasize economic issues. Even on shared priorities such as education, Hispanics and non-Hispanics often have different objectives. In the 2000 presidential race, for example, the educational concerns of whites focused on measures of teacher and student assessment, while Hispanics stressed the process of education, including school overcrowding and the need for culturally sensitive curricula. Local races in which funding for or access to education is central to the debate witness disproportionate increases in Hispanic turnout.

Compared with whites, Hispanics also express greater trust in government, which partly explains their support for higher taxes to expand government programs. Cubans report the highest levels of trust in the U.S. government, probably because of the special concessions they have enjoyed as political refugees, but differences in trust among other Hispanic subgroups are relatively small. Equally noteworthy is the low priority accorded to ethnic specific issues, such as bilingual education or U.S. relations with Latin America. Although Hispanics share with other racial and ethnic groups concerns about the volume of contemporary migration, their focus is not on stemming those flows but on fair treatment regardless of legal status. Finally, the major issues defining the conservative moral agenda—abortion, family values, and the death penalty—are rarely mentioned as important issues among Hispanics.[33] Nonetheless, preliminary evidence from the 2004 election shows that such issues can be framed to mobilize Hispanics selectively and further divide them along partisan lines.[34]

While Hispanics hold strong views on many social issues, their levels of participation in electoral, civic, and organizational activities fall well below those of whites or blacks (with the notable exception of self-reported parental involvement in school-based activities). Hispanics are less likely than whites to be members of community-based organizations and to donate time or money to civic activities in their communities. And fewer Hispanics assume leadership roles in civic organizations than do whites or blacks.[35]

Some preliminary evidence suggests that Hispanics' involvement in the politics of their home countries or communities serves as a precursor to their civic involvement in the United States. Hispanic immigrants are increasingly participating in transnational civic activities; the best estimate suggests that approximately 20 percent of Hispanic immigrants engage in such activities. However, this participation declines with longer periods of residence and once a migrant's immediate family has fully migrated to the United States.

The gap between the growth of the Hispanic population and its voting numbers has been developing for some time, but has widened considerably in recent years.[36] Surveys of voter registration and turnout consistently show lower rates for Hispanics—approximately 10 percentage points below those for blacks and 15 points below those for whites—over the last 25 years. For the 2004 election, approximately 58 percent of Hispanic citizens were registered to vote, and 47 percent voted; the comparable figures for whites were 75 and 67 percent. Voting among Hispanics has increased only marginally over the last 20 years despite considerable growth in outreach to potential Hispanic voters.

The voting gap between registered Hispanic and non-Hispanic citizens largely parallels group differences in characteristics that are correlated with electoral participation. Simply put, poor, young citizens with low educational levels, even if registered to vote, are significantly less likely to cast ballots than well-educated, affluent seniors. Additional factors responsible for low Hispanic voter turnout include institutional arrangements and past exclusion, but their impact cannot be assessed accurately with available data.[37]

Foreign-born Hispanics, even naturalized citizens, are less likely to become involved in civic and nonelectoral political activities than Hispanics who are U.S. citizens by birth. More generally, cultural assimilation appears to foster political engagement: civic involvement increases with longer periods of U.S. residence, with third-generation Hispanics voting at higher rates than their second-generation counterparts.[38] Still, low rates of naturalization among the foreign-born dampen Hispanics' electoral participation relative to whites. Over the last three decades, as immigration has fueled Hispanic population growth, each new Hispanic voter has essentially been matched by one nonvoter and nearly two adult noncitizens. For political activities that require citizenship for participation, therefore, the immigrant-heavy population composition of Hispanics not only tempers their political influence at the ballot box, but also renders predictions about their future political behavior highly uncertain.

Moreover, political office holding by Hispanics has barely kept pace with demographic growth. Despite some high-profile Hispanic victories—such as Antonio Villaraigosa's defeat of incumbent James Hahn in the 2005 Los Angeles mayoral race—Hispanics' representation in elected offices relative to their population size has not increased since the 1970s. With a significantly larger and increasingly more geographically dispersed population, Hispanics' low levels of voter turnout and political office holding have more profound implications for representation and governance now than in the past.

If Hispanics are to use politics effectively in advancing their social and economic interests, two conditions must be met: their rates of civic engagement, particularly at the ballot box and in elected positions, must increase, and democratic institutions must be more responsive to their demands. Because large numbers of Hispanics are not citizens and hence cannot vote, their success in expressing political views requires mobilization beyond the ballot box, such as coalition politics, representation through community-based organizations, and alignment with interest groups supporting the politics of inclusion. Districting strategies that maximize the likelihood of electing Hispanics to influential positions can help by strengthening Hispanics' political influence.

Los Angeles offers a clear example of these conditions. Over the past 20 years, the Hispanic share of the city electorate has more than doubled, in part because of a surge in naturalization during the late 1990s and early 2000s. Yet the large numbers of youth and noncitizens among the voting-age population means that the Hispanic share of the city's electorate is less than half their share of the city's population. Mayor Villaraigosa's victory required a coalition of Hispanics, blacks, and whites.

Given the many uncertainties faced by Hispanics in the demographic, economic, and social realms (see Chapter 6), their political future is highly uncertain. It is possible that some catalyst—such as the anti-immigrant provisions of the 1996 welfare reform law—will cause large numbers of Hispanic adults who now either do not vote, or as noncitizens are ineligible to vote, to become citizens and participate in the political process. Alternatively, Hispanics' current passive attitude toward politics may persist, resulting in limited success in recruiting new voters—particularly the young, second generation. Should this scenario play out, parties and candidates would likely lose interest in Hispanics' political mobilization.

The most plausible scenario, however, is that the Hispanic electorate will continue to grow incrementally over successive election cycles and will maintain some distinctive features relative to the non-Hispanic electorate. Even slow incremental growth in the Hispanic electorate raises the possibility that Hispanics will become a critical swing constituency that decides future electoral outcomes, as was the case in Los Angeles in 2005. The 2004 election clearly demonstrated that Republicans can make inroads into Hispanic electorates; so, too, can Democrats, as they did among traditionally Republican Florida Hispanics. Yet neither population size nor electorate strength can guarantee influence or political voice. To be influential as a bloc, Hispanics will have to build and maintain political cohesiveness.

CONCLUSION

For Hispanics, as with other immigrant groups, the challenges of integration include social and economic mobility and the development of an effective political voice. Contemporary conditions, such as the changing social contract, economic trends, and the aging of the white majority—along with the geographic dispersal of Hispanic communities—both define these challenges and present both risks and opportunities for successful integration of native- and foreign-born Hispanics.

Economic trends that reduce the demand for less-skilled workers pose formidable risks, especially for prospective workers. The Hispanic age boomlet poses a potential demographic dividend that can partially offset the rising burden of dependency of the aging white majority. In the political arena, Hispanics are potentially influential because of their growing numbers and residential dispersion, but low rates of civil engagement continue to limit their collective voice.

How these aspects of Hispanic integration into U.S. society will play out into the foreseeable future remains highly uncertain. The next chapter examines key dimensions of the Hispanic experience that will play a major role in how these uncertainties are resolved.

NOTES

1 Weber et al., 2004.

2 Looff and Associates, 1999:Tables 3-11 and 3-12.

3 Tyson, 2004.

4 Danziger and Gottschalk, 1995; Freeman, 1993; Levy, 1995, 1998.

5 Borjas, 2003; Card, 2001; Massey et al., 2002.

6 Danziger, 2004:2-3; Wolff, 2004.

7 Danziger, 2004:2-3.

8 Levy, 1995, 1998; Levy and Murnane, 2004.

9 Levy and Murnane, 2004.

10 Levy and Murnane, 2004.

11 Duncan et al., 2006.

12 Generational status cannot be estimated readily from the U.S. census because the parentage question that identified birthplace of parents was eliminated in 1980. However, this information is available in the Current Population Survey, which is based on a sample rather than a full enumeration—hence the "estimate" rather than enumerated generational composition. "Third generation" includes a substantial share of persons of fourth, fifth, and higher-order generational status.

13 See Passel, 2004, op. cit. These estimates differ slightly from published census statistics because they are based on backward projections.

14 Watson Wyatt Worldwide, 2004. This study claims that capital and technological investments will help increase productivity but cannot fully offset labor shortfalls, and vice versa. Fehr et al., 2004, argue that immigration by itself does little to mitigate the fiscal stresses associated with the aging of industrialized societies, but the potential benefits will be even less in the absence of human capital investment in either immigrants or their second-generation offspring.

15 Porter, 2005.

16 Kandel and Cromartie, 2004.

17 Logan et al., 2004.

18 Logan, 2003.

19 Fischer and Tienda, 2006.

20 Logan, 2003. For U.S.-born Hispanics, the averages are slightly lower—28 percent and 50 percent, respectively.

21 Davis, 2003; Olson and Jordon, 2003.

22 Ginsburg and Moberg, 2004.

23 See Fischer and Tienda, 2006.

24 See Fischer and Tienda, 2006.

25 This is well dramatized in the documentary, *Farmingville*, but is being replayed in many other communities that witnessed significant increases in their Hispanic population during the 1990s, such as Danbury, Connecticut and Herndon, Virginia.

26 Orfield et al., 2004.

27 Kochhar et al., 2005.

28 Myers et al., 2002.

29 Wolff, 2004.

30 Pew Hispanic Center, 2004.

31 National Council of La Raza, 2004.

32 DeSipio, 2006.

33 de la Garza et al., 1992:88-90, 141, 166-171, 193; Henry J. Kaiser Family Foundation, 2002:42-43.

34 Louis DeSipio, personal communication, November 2004.

35 Verba et al., 1995.

36 Suro et al., 2005.

37 See DeSipio, 2006.

38 See DeSipio et al., 2003. Small sample sizes in surveys require some caution in generalization.

Freddy Rodriquez
Hasta Cuando (1991), *Chapita/Bottlecaps* (1990)
Copyright by the artist; used with permission.

5

Realms of Integration:
Family, Education, Work, and Health

This chapter examines four aspects of the Hispanic experience—family and living arrangements; schools and education; employment and economic well-being; and health status and access to care. These attributes not only portray current terms of belonging, but also highlight risks and opportunities that will ultimately define the future of the U.S. Hispanic population. A focus on features that set Hispanics apart from other groups—notably language use, youthfulness, and large shares of unskilled immigrants—helps assess whether the identified risks are likely to be enduring.

FAMILY AND LIVING ARRANGEMENTS[1]

Hispanic families are often extolled as a source of strength and cohesion that derives from their "familism"—a strong commitment to family life that values collective goals over individual well-being. Indicators of familism that differentiate Hispanics from whites include early childbearing and higher average fertility levels, large family households that often extend beyond nuclear members, and a greater overall tendency to live with kin rather than with unrelated individuals or alone. As a source of support for relatives in the extended network of kin relationships, familism can help mitigate economic and social risks in the face of adversity. These sentiments were echoed across the generational spectrum in focus groups conducted for the panel:

> Sometimes families here, white families, are not as united as Hispanic families are. We're always famous for having aunts and uncles and relatives. Americans, it's just mom and dad and kids. (Mexican immigrant, Raleigh)

* * *

> Typically, we have close families. Family is a really big part of our culture. (third-generation Hispanic, Houston)

At the same time, consistent with their varied immigration histories and social conditions, Hispanic families are highly diverse. Specific aspects of family behavior, such as intermarriage patterns, cohesion among relatives, and the content of social exchanges, differ by nationality and generation. Mexican Americans are considered particularly familistic, possibly because the large numbers of immigrants among them bring cultural traditions into sharper relief.

Most observers agree that the positive aspects of familism are worth keeping, yet there is no consensus on what can be preserved in the face of the rapid Americanization of second-generation youth. Whether ideals of collective support and other positive features of familism will endure and what forms family structure among Hispanics will take in the future are open questions with far-reaching implications for the evolution of group identity and social well-being.

If Hispanics follow the paths of other immigrant groups, their familism would appear to be in jeopardy as they acculturate, experience socio-economic mobility, and adopt U.S. norms, which includes many behaviors that tend to erode kinship patterns and traditional family behavior. The rise in divorce and nonmarital childbearing among Hispanics, evident in the growth of mother-only families, signals what some scholars term "family decline."[2] In 1980, fathers were absent in 12 percent of white families, 38 percent of both Dominican and Puerto Rican families, and 40 percent of black families. By 2000, approximately 14 percent of white families had a single female head, compared with about 20 percent of Mexican and Cuban families, 25 percent of Central and South American families, 36 percent of Dominican and Puerto Rican families, and 45 percent of black families.[3] Because mother-only families are significantly more likely to be poor, this trend signals new vulnerabilities for the growing numbers of youths reared by single parents.

Generational transitions also dilute familism, although apparently not uniformly among Hispanic subgroups. For example, among Mexicans and

Puerto Ricans born in the United States, the percentage of married-couple households is smaller and the percentage of female-headed households larger than among first-generation immigrants. Compared with the immigrant generation, U.S.-born Mexican Americans exhibit higher divorce rates. Only 56 percent of third-generation Mexican children (those who have American-born parents) live with both parents, compared with about 73 percent of children with Mexican-born parents. Another sign of dwindling familism is the shrinking size of extended families, which often results in reduced safety nets for related individuals.[4]

Rising nonmarital childbearing is another sign of eroding Hispanic familism. Between 1980 and 2000, the percentage of births to unmarried women more than doubled for whites (134 percent), Mexicans (101 percent), and Cubans (173 percent), and increased by more than half for Central and South Americans (64 percent) and other Hispanics (97 percent). Out-of-wedlock childbearing among Puerto Ricans rose more slowly because, as with blacks, their share of nonmarital births was already high in 1980. By 2000, the percentage of births to unmarried Hispanic mothers was between that of whites (22 percent) and blacks (69 percent). The rate for Cubans was closer to that for whites at 27 percent, and the Puerto Rican rate was closer to that for blacks, at 59 percent. At 44 percent, the out-of-wedlock birth rate for Central and South Americans lay between the extremes.

Finally, the cultural mergers produced by rising rates of intermarriage— between Hispanics and non-Hispanics and among Hispanic nationalities— can diminish or redefine the content of familism. As a measure of social distance between groups, an indicator of assimilation, and a force that shapes racial and ethnic boundaries, intermarriage can either redefine or erode Hispanic familism over generations. For all Hispanics, the tendency to marry, cohabit, and procreate with members of their own ethnic group declines across generations, though notable differences exist across groups. Mexican Americans not only are considered to be more familistic than other Hispanics, but also, given their large numbers, are far more likely to be paired with a member of the same ethnic group in marriage, cohabitation, or parenthood than are Puerto Ricans, Cubans, Central/South Americans, or other Hispanics.[5] One possible explanation for this is that high levels of immigration, buttressed by residential segregation, help preserve Mexican familism in the face of erosion from other sources.

Whether traditional Hispanic familistic orientations will persist beyond the third generation, whether they will take the same forms, and whether they will serve similar protective functions is unknown. Trends in marriage, cohabitation, and parenthood offer provocative insights. Hispanics are more likely to partner with another Hispanic in marriage than in cohabitation and nonmarital parenthood. Although generally less common, relationships with white partners frequently involve marriage. U.S.-born Hispanics are more likely than Hispanic immigrants to have a white, or other non-Hispanic, spouse.[6] Unions among partners of different Hispanic origins or between Hispanics and blacks are more likely to involve cohabitation and unmarried childbearing. Hispanic-black unions quite frequently produce children out of wedlock.

Hispanics' interethnic unions foreshadow changing ethnic boundaries through childbearing. In particular, children of mixed unions face complex identity issues: Will they retain a mixed identity, adopt the ethnic (or racial) identity of one parent, or perhaps opt for a panethnic identity? Unions between Hispanic women and white partners can facilitate assimilation into mainstream white society, because these mixed marriages are more common among the better educated. Whether and how Hispanics' ethnic mixing will redraw racial and ethnic boundaries in the United States is uncertain because the prevalence of intermarriage depends on even greater uncertainties, such as the effect of geographic dispersal on the incidence of mixed unions, future levels of immigration, and the way persons of mixed ancestry self-identify ethnically.[7] Because of their sheer numbers and relatively high residential concentration, Mexican Americans are likely to retain a relatively distinct ethnic identity, although generational transitions will blur boundaries though unions with whites. Smaller in size, other Hispanic sub-groups are less likely to sustain discrete identities over time because of their higher levels of ethnic mixing with other Hispanic groups and with blacks, which creates greater ambiguity about the place of their offspring in the evolving racial spectrum. How settlement patterns recontour marriage markets will also decide the viability of Hispanicity as a panethnic identity.

SCHOOLS AND EDUCATION[8]

The United States houses some of the most outstanding universities in the world, which coexist with countless highly dysfunctional primary and secondary schools. Thousands of young Hispanics must pursue inter- and intragenerational social mobility predominantly via segregated inner-city schools that feature dropout rates well above the national average. The vastly unequal opportunities for academic achievement they confront in the lower grades contribute to widening disparities at higher levels of the education system.

Although most demographic groups have experienced significant increases in educational attainment since the 1960s, Hispanics are distinguished by their historically low levels of completed schooling, currently completing less formal schooling than any other demographic group.[9] In the context of the rising demand for skills in today's economy, this liability is cause for concern.

In 2000 working-age Hispanics averaged nearly 3 years less of formal schooling than U.S.-born whites and blacks. Moreover, there are large disparities in educational attainment among Hispanic groups, mainly between the native- and foreign-born. On average, foreign-born Hispanics of working age complete 2.5 years less of formal schooling than their U.S.-born compatriots, with negligible differences between men and women. As Figure 5-1 shows, the educational standing of foreign-born Hispanics has eroded since 1980 compared with both whites and blacks. By contrast,

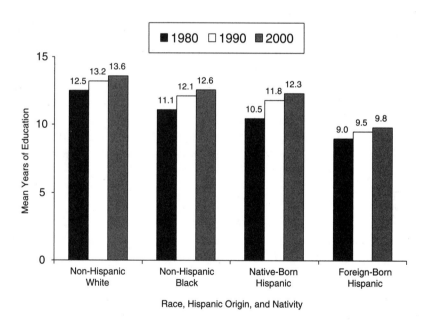

FIGURE 5-1 Mean years of education by race/ethnicity and nativity, 1980-2000.
NOTE: For ages 25 to 64.
SOURCE: U.S. Bureau of the Census (2000b), Integrated Public Use Microdata Series (IPUMS) 1 percent samples for 1980-2000.

U.S.-born Hispanics have closed the school attainment gap with whites by more than half a year—from 2 to 1.3 years over the same period.

Educational disparities between foreign- and native-born Hispanics play out as inequities among national-origin groups of working age because of the changing volume and composition of immigration in recent decades (see Chapter 2). Not only do foreign-born Mexicans feature the lowest educational levels of any Hispanic subgroup, but the gap in completed schooling between the foreign and native born is larger for Mexicans than for Hispanics of other nationalities—rising from 3 years in 1980 to 4.4 years in 2000—owing to substantial educational advances among the U.S.-born rather than declining attainment of recent immigrants (see Figure 5-2). For other Hispanics, the birthplace gap in education rose more modestly during the same period—from 1 to 1.6 years—while for Puerto Ricans it was reduced by half. Cubans are distinguished from other Hispanic ethnicities because their average education level exceeds that of other sub-groups, because foreign-born Cubans average more schooling than native-born Hispanics, and because the educational attainment of U.S.-born Cubans equals (in the case of men) or surpasses (in the case of women) that of white men and women.[10]

If the schooling deficits of foreign-born Hispanics are imported from Latin America, the disparities among the native-born are produced in the United States. Scholastic disadvantages result from a myriad of social and family circumstances—mainly low parental education levels—and are compounded by schools that fail to deliver quality education.[11] Fortunately, educational disadvantages can be prevented for Hispanic youths that have not yet begun their school careers and reversed for those already enrolled.

Early Beginnings

Hispanic students' educational disadvantages begin in the early grades for two main reasons—their delayed entry into formal school settings and their limited opportunities to acquire preliteracy skills. Parents of Hispanic preschoolers are less likely than black, white, or Asian parents to be fluent in English and, because many have poor educational levels themselves, to have the resources necessary to promote their children's prescholastic literacy. This is highly significant because reading to preschool children fosters their language acquisition, enhances their early reading performance and social development, and may promote their future academic success.

Participation in home literacy activities such as telling stories or visit-

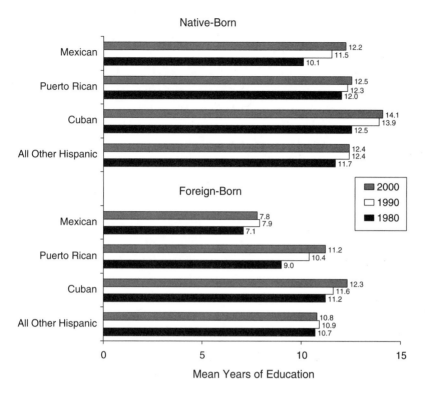

FIGURE 5-2 Mean years of education of Hispanics by ethnicity.
NOTE: For ages 25 to 64.
SOURCE: U.S. Bureau of the Census (2000b), Integrated Public Use Microdata Series (IPUMS) 1 percent samples for 1980-2000.

ing libraries is especially low for children reared in Spanish-dominant homes. In 1999, children of Spanish monolinguals were only half as likely as white children to participate in such activities; if both parents were fluent in English, the gap was just 15 percentage points. The lack of exposure to preschool literacy activities, particularly among children from Spanish-dominant households, often creates literacy disadvantages in the early grades. A 1999 study by the U.S. Department of Education showed that Hispanic kindergarten students trailed their Asian and other non-Hispanic classmates in both reading and math skills.[12] Only Native American students had lower preschool reading literacy rates than Hispanics whose parents spoke little English (although Hispanic children exhibited lower math skills).

Household language partly reflects social class divisions and recent immigrant status—two attributes that influence children's exposure to literacy activities before kindergarten. Yet differences in school readiness between Hispanic youth reared in Spanish-dominant homes and English-dominant homes are not an indictment of Spanish-language use per se. Moreover, programs such as Head Start appear to raise Hispanic children's low average preschool literacy rates. Yet quality preschool programs often are either unavailable where the neediest children live or too costly for family budgets. Thus disadvantaged Hispanic children are left to make their way in the public schools, increasing their vulnerability to failure in the years ahead.

Primary and Middle Years

The academic achievement gap evident when Hispanics first enter school continues through the primary grades. During the first two years, teachers' perceptions of their Hispanic students' academic abilities often skew scholastic assessments, regardless of the children's actual aptitude. Results of the Early Childhood Longitudinal Study revealed that kindergarten teachers systematically rated Hispanic students below white students when first enrolled. As Hispanic children performed above their teachers' initial expectations, the gap between test-based abilities and teacher assessments decreased by half to two-thirds during kindergarten and was eliminated by the end of the first grade. Such teacher biases are compounded by a shortage of staff who understand Hispanic children's cultural backgrounds. Nationally, Hispanic students constitute approximately 15 percent of elementary school students—and nearly 20 percent of all school-age students—yet only 4 percent of public school teachers are Hispanic.[13]

Although Hispanic elementary school children have made steady progress in reading and math, greater gains by other groups have sustained or in some cases widened Hispanic achievement gaps. A 20-year comparison of test scores reported in the National Assessment of Educational Progress shows that Hispanic students continue to lag behind whites in their scholastic achievement throughout middle and high school.[14] Evident for all Hispanic subgroups, these gaps are decidedly largest for Mexican Americans, the fastest-growing segment of the elementary school population. Carried into future grades, accumulating deficits in literacy and math competencies inhibit the learning of other academic subjects.

Middle school Hispanic students often encounter two circumstances that limit their chances for scholastic success: large, urban schools, generally considered suboptimal for learning in the middle grades,[15] and weak ties with their teachers.[16] Weak relations with teachers diminish students' motivation to pursue academic work, and in turn lower teachers' expectations in a self-perpetuating cycle of academic disengagement and under-achievement. That students who become disengaged from school during the middle years cannot well appreciate the practical relevance of what is being taught in the classroom bodes ill for their academic performance in high school and dampens their aspirations for college.

Secondary School and Beyond

Even under optimal circumstances, the transition from middle to high school is a taxing experience for most students. This passage is especially difficult for Hispanic and black adolescents destined for oversized, resource-poor urban high schools staffed with many inexperienced or uncertified teachers.[17] Moreover, students whose parents lack a high school education are most in need of early guidance in course planning and preparation for college. Such guidance is in short supply in the schools these students attend. Given their parents' limited experience with the U.S. educational system and the blind trust many Hispanic parents are willing to place in teachers' authority, Hispanic eighth graders are more likely than any other demographic group to express uncertainty about the classes they will take in high school.[18] Mexican immigrant parents are especially likely to defer to teachers and administrators, rarely questioning their decisions.

High school experiences are vital in shaping students' educational expectations and occupational aspirations. Yet a recent study found that, compared with 25 percent of blacks, 31 percent of whites, and 37 percent of Asian Americans, only 23 percent of Hispanic eighth graders planned to enroll in a college preparatory curriculum.[19] These findings underscore the urgency of effective counseling on course selection in secondary school, particularly for students whose parents may be unfamiliar with the complexities of the U.S. educational system.

Despite modest improvements in recent years, rates of school failure among Hispanics remain unacceptably high. Even counting only those who actually attended U.S. high schools, the share of Hispanic high school students 16 to 19 years old who failed to graduate fell only marginally during the 1990s, from 22 to 21 percent.[20] The numbers involved are sobering because the school-age population in the United States has been growing rapidly as the children of baby boomers and recent immigrants make their way through the education system. That dropout rates for whites and blacks fell even more than for Hispanics—from 10 to 8 percent and from 14 to 12 percent, respectively—widened racial and ethnic disparities in secondary school success. Nor is the General Equivalency Diploma (GED) a viable route for Hispanics to close their high school achievement gap. In 1998, 7.9 percent of white 18- to 29-year-olds achieved high school equivalence by passing the GED test, as compared with 7 percent of Hispanics.[21] Moreover, those with exam-certified high school equivalency fare no better in the labor market than high school dropouts.[22]

Although foreign-born Hispanic youths ages 16 to 19 are significantly more likely than those who are native born to leave high school without a diploma—34 versus 14 percent in 2000—being foreign born is not the main factor explaining their failure to graduate. Many are recent arrivals who were already behind in school before arriving in the U.S.[23] Once here, they are likely to attend urban schools—such as those in Los Angeles, Chicago, and New York—that serve large numbers of low-income minority students and for which low graduation rates are typical. Fully 40 percent of Hispanic students attend high schools that graduate less than 60 percent of entering freshmen.[24]

Popular allegations that Hispanics value education less than do other groups are contradicted by evidence that large numbers of Hispanic high school students aspire to attend college. A study conducted by Public Agenda, a New York-based nonprofit public opinion research organization, found that 65 percent of Hispanic parents, compared with 47 percent of black and 33 percent of white parents, believed a college education is the single most important factor for economic success.[25] Yet Hispanics trail all other groups in their ambitions to pursue 4-year college degrees because of their disadvantaged beginnings, limited home educational resources, concentration in scholastically weak high schools, and lack of concrete information about how to prepare for college.[26]

Compared with whites and blacks, more second-generation Hispanic youths are the first in their family to attend college. But college prospects are limited for many because they fail to take courses or exams required for college entrance—another consequence of their poor guidance counseling during high school. Compared with other subjects, achievement in mathematics is the strongest predictor of college enrollment. That Hispanic students are about 20 percent less likely than whites to complete advanced mathematics, as well as less likely than both whites and blacks to take advanced science courses, compromises their post–high school educational options.[27]

Hispanic high school graduates are also less likely than whites, Asians, and blacks to take college entrance examinations or apply to college.[28] Spanish-language use per se does not explain this gap because bilingual Hispanics are more likely than whites to complete Advanced Placement courses and to take College Board exams. And parents who are proficient in both English and Spanish often can advance their children's educational prospects by bridging cultural and language divides.[29]

Despite the above obstacles, college enrollment among Hispanics has been on the rise. There is evidence that Hispanic high school graduates are more likely than white or black students to enroll in some form of college, but Hispanics also are significantly less likely to obtain a 4-year degree because they are more likely to enroll in 2-year colleges, to attend college only part-time, or to work while enrolled full-time.[30] This is especially true for Mexicans. In 2000, Hispanics were 11 percent of high school graduates.[31] They accounted for only 7 percent of students enrolled in 4-year institutions, but 14 percent of enrollees in 2-year colleges. Differences in college attendance between native- and foreign-born Hispanics contribute somewhat to these outcomes, but they are not the driving force.

Major reasons why Hispanics are more likely than whites to enroll in 2-year rather than 4-year colleges are poor academic preparation, weak counseling, and cost. Hispanics from Spanish-speaking families (for whom the risks of dropping out of high school are higher) are nearly as likely as blacks to attend 4-year colleges if they receive adequate academic preparation.[32] Like many students who begin their college careers at community colleges, Hispanics intend to transfer to 4-year institutions, but they are less successful than other groups in making the transition.[33] Furthermore, enrollment in a 4-year institution does not guarantee a degree. Compared with other high-achieving youths who enroll in 4-year institutions, Hispanics are less likely to receive baccalaureate degrees, unless they are among the select few who attend a highly selective college.[34]

ECONOMIC WELL-BEING

As in so many other ways, Hispanics are highly diverse with respect to economic well-being. On the one hand, lacking the protections afforded by legal status, millions of undocumented Hispanics fill low-wage jobs; many make ends meet by holding multiple jobs and pooling incomes from several household members. On the other hand, rising rates of home ownership attest that both established immigrants and native-born citizens are increasingly joining the ranks of the middle class.[35] This section reviews two aspects of economic well-being—employment and earnings, and household income—among Hispanics, as well as their experience of the extremes of poverty and wealth.

Employment and Earnings[36]

Hispanics' success in the U.S. labor market depends on their propensity to work, their skills, the kinds of jobs they secure, and, because many U.S. employers discount human capital acquired abroad, where they were born (see Figure 5-3).[37] On average, Hispanic men's employment rate (87 percent) is somewhat lower than that for U.S.-born whites (92 percent), but well above that for U.S.-born blacks (77 percent).[38] Also among men, the average employment rate for both Cubans and Mexicans (both foreign- and U.S.-born) is similar to that for whites, but that for Puerto Rican men is appreciably lower, while that for island-born Puerto Ricans is similar to that for U.S.-born blacks.[39]

Birthplace differences in employment rates are much larger for Hispanic women than men. Overall, some 61 percent of immigrant Hispanic women were employed in 2000, compared with 76 percent of their U.S.-born counterparts. With just over one in two employed, Mexican immigrants have the lowest employment rate of all women, but the rate for island-born Puerto Ricans is only slightly higher at 61 percent. Average employment rates for U.S.-born Mexicans and Puerto Ricans are close to those for blacks (78 percent) and whites (80 percent), while Cubans have the highest rate of all, at 83 percent.

Owing to differences in educational attainment and language skills between native- and foreign-born Hispanics, the types of jobs they hold vary more on this dimension than by nationality. Foreign-born Hispanic men work disproportionately in agriculture (11 percent) and construction (18 percent), while foreign-born Hispanic women are overrepresented in manufacturing (19 percent)—mainly in production of nondurable goods.[40] Consistent with their education and English-language skills, Hispanic men and women born abroad are underrepresented in managerial/professional and technical/sales occupations, and overrepresented in service and operator/laborer occupations.

Men

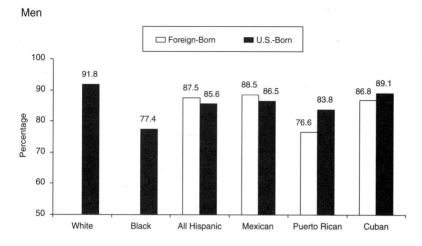

Women

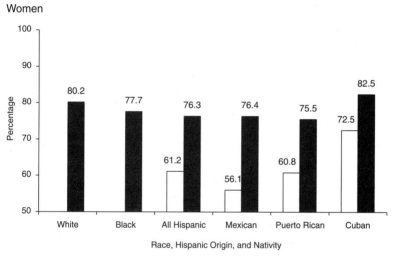

Race, Hispanic Origin, and Nativity

FIGURE 5-3 Employment rates for white, black, and Hispanic men and women ages 25-59 by nativity.
SOURCE: U.S. Bureau of the Census (2000b), 5 percent samples Integrated Public Use Microdata Series (IPUMS).

Hispanics' lower levels of education and English proficiency largely explain their lower employment rates compared with whites.[41] The 6 percentage point employment gap between native-born Mexican and white men would narrow to a mere 2 percentage points if their education and language skills were similar. With education and English proficiency levels comparable to those of whites, the employment rates of foreign-born Mexican immigrants also would be similar.[42] Foreign-born Mexican women provide an even more dramatic example, as their average employment deficit of 25 percentage points would shrink to just 3 with education and English proficiency levels comparable to those of white women. Puerto Ricans and Dominicans are an exception to this pattern because sizable employment gaps persist for them even with human capital endowments comparable to those of whites.[43]

On average, native-born Hispanic men earned 31 percent and foreign-born Hispanic men 59 percent less than whites in 1999. With similar human capital endowments, those earnings gaps would shrink to 13 and 5 percent, respectively. By comparison, and despite their higher average education levels and better command of English relative to Hispanics, black men suffer a 44 percent earnings penalty. Foreign-born Hispanic women earn about half as much as white women on average, but this disparity, too, would shrink given comparable educational attainment and English fluency.

Hispanics' average earnings also differ by national origin. Native-born Cubans enjoy relatively high earnings: U.S.-born Cuban men earn as much as white men, and native-born Cuban women earn 20 percent *more* than white women. By contrast, both Mexicans and Puerto Ricans—especially those born abroad—exhibit large gaps compared with whites. But if Mexican and Puerto Rican women born abroad—whose average earnings trail those of white women by 63 and 28 percent, respectively—were as fluent in English and as well educated as white women, their earnings gaps would virtually disappear.[44] Legal status also affects wages, with legal immigrants earning substantially more than those who are undocumented, and wage inequality, as discussed below.[45]

Thus unlike black men, for whom continuing discrimination in the labor market creates and augments earnings disparities, Hispanics could dramatically reduce their earnings gap with whites by closing the education gap and becoming proficient in English.[46] This does not mean that Hispanics do not experience discrimination in the labor market. There is some evidence of differences in treatment at initial contact and interview and in outcomes based on accent and phenotype.[47]

To understand the origins of earnings differentials and accurately portray Hispanic socioeconomic progress over time, one must consider changes in the birthplace composition of the Hispanic workforce. Since 1980, high rates of immigration have changed the human capital profile of Hispanic workers and widened their earnings disparities with whites. For example, the foreign-born share among Mexican men aged 25 to 59 surged from 37 percent in 1980 to 51 percent in 1990 and 63 percent in 2000. Among Hispanics, Mexicans are the largest ethnic group, average the lowest levels of human capital, and include a sizable share of undocumented workers.[48] With average educational attainment levels of 12 years for the native born and less than 9 years for the foreign born, Mexicans have faced particularly bleak labor market prospects since 1980, as the wage premiums for high skills grew and income inequality widened.

Looking back six decades, in 1940 Mexican men earned just over half (56 percent) of white men's wages. That figure rose to nearly 70 percent in the postwar decade, a period of vigorous economic growth when strong unions protected the wages of laborers. Although the Mexican-white earnings gap remained unchanged during the next two decades, by 1990 Mexican men's wages had deteriorated to 45 percent of those of white men, and this gap persisted through the following decade.[49] By contrast, earnings of black men rose between 1990 and 2000, from 50 to 56 percent of white male earnings. Larger human capital gaps since 1980, especially among the foreign born, are responsible for the stagnation of Hispanic earnings through 2000, especially as the premium placed on work-related skills has continued to rise.[50]

Previous waves of predominantly unskilled immigrants, such as the Irish and Italians, enjoyed substantial intergenerational progress that ultimately enabled their descendants to join the middle class. For most, though, this process required two or three generations to accomplish; moreover, the skill endowments of the immigrant generation were instrumental in the labor market success of their children and grandchildren.[51] Generational comparisons are particularly instructive for envisioning possible economic destinies for Hispanics. But because Hispanic immigrants are so diverse with respect to their length of U.S. residence, and because native-born Hispanics represent multiple generations, comparisons by birthplace are too coarse to portray true intergenerational progress. Snapshots of the Hispanic population taken over time can only approximate such progress, but nonetheless provide rough measures of the direction and pace of change.

Substantial educational gains realized by the U.S.-born offspring of Hispanic immigrants have narrowed the white-Hispanic earnings gap across generations, with the most sizable convergence occurring between the first and second generations. A smaller wage convergence occurs between the second and third generations, which mirrors the apparent stagnation of Hispanics' educational progress relative to whites. For example, for the

1998-2000 period, the earnings gap between Mexican and white men dropped from 66 percent for immigrants to 38 percent for the second generation and 31 percent for the third and subsequent generations combined. Second-generation Mexicans even reaped higher earnings than native-born black men with higher levels of education. Earnings deficits for Puerto Rican men were 46 percent for the first generation, 30 percent for the second generation, and 16 percent for later generations. Reflecting their higher-class origins at arrival, Cuban immigrants' 31 percent initial deficit disappeared by the second generation.[52]

The apparent slowdown in Hispanic socioeconomic progress after the second generation may be more imagined than real because it is impossible to match immigrant parents and grandparents of the first generation with their descendants in later generations.[53] In fact, substantial educational and earnings gains are evident when second-generation Hispanics are compared with their third-generation descendants 25 years later. For example, one study showed that not only are schooling gaps smaller in the second compared with the first generation, but they are always lower in the third generation.[54]

Educational gains of younger third-generation relative to older second-generation Hispanics are an encouraging sign of intergenerational progress, but they yield conservative estimates of mobility for two reasons. First, the pace of intergenerational progress may be more rapid than available data can accurately portray because of the uncertain volume, pace, and composition of immigrant flows. Decennial censuses can only approximate this highly dynamic process, which for Hispanics is further complicated by the presence of a large and growing undocumented population, whose integration prospects are highly uncertain. Second, selective opting out of Hispanic ethnicity by third and higher generations would lead to underestimation of intergenerational progress. If the most successful Hispanics are less likely to identify themselves or their children as Hispanic—either because they are more likely to marry non-Hispanics or for other reasons—available estimates of earnings gains achieved between the second and third generations are conservative. Studies focused on documenting the prevalence of such opting out of Hispanic identity are relatively recent, and consensus on this issue has not yet been established.[55]

Recent evidence for Mexicans supports the idea that the most economically assimilated Hispanics—predominantly those from the third and higher generations—may be less likely to self-identify as Hispanic.[56] U.S.-born Mexican Americans who marry non-Mexicans are substantially more educated, on average, than Mexican Americans who marry within their ethnic group (either U.S. or foreign born), as their higher employment levels and earnings attest. Moreover, the children of intermarried Mexican Americans are much less likely to self-identify as Mexican than are the children of two Mexican parents. This implies that children of Mexican-origin parents with low education, employment, and earnings may be more likely to self-identify as Mexican than the offspring of intermarriage, which would bias downward assessments of Mexican Americans' intergenerational progress beyond the second generation. The magnitude of such biases, however, has yet to be systematically assessed.[57]

Given these uncertainties, conclusions about intergenerational changes in the labor market experience of Hispanics remain tentative at best. The evidence is clear as to improvement in educational attainment and earnings growth between first- and second-generation Hispanics, both absolutely and relative to whites. But the evidence regarding progress between the second and third generations, and especially beyond the third, is less clear, because educational gains between the second and third generations are not matched by commensurate progress in earnings, particularly among younger Mexicans.[58] Less debatable is that deficiencies in education and language skills will remain a formidable obstacle to the labor market success of Hispanics, especially for immigrants, and will continue to hamper their economic progress—perhaps even more so in the years ahead than in the past—because of the higher premium placed on skills and because blue-collar jobs that traditionally served as gateways to the middle class have all but vanished. Whether the growing second generation makes sufficient progress in closing these two key obstacles to economic mobility will be decisive in the long-term positioning of the Hispanic population.

Household Income

For obvious reasons, the gaps in employment and earnings experienced by Hispanics are reflected in disparities in household income. On average, incomes of white households are larger than those of Hispanic households, just how much larger depending on the birthplace and ethnicity of the Hispanic householder. Again mirroring employment and earnings disparities, U.S.-born Hispanic householders of all national origins garner higher incomes than blacks, although this pattern does not hold for households headed by immigrants. In 1999, the median income of Hispanic households was just about 70 percent that of whites and about 10 percent higher than that of blacks.[59] At the top of the Hispanic household income ladder are South Americans and Cubans who were either born or raised in the United States.[60] Ranking lowest on median household income, as with most other measures of economic well-being, are Puerto Ricans and Dominicans, followed by Mexicans (see Figure 5-4).

As noted, an obvious explanation for the low household incomes of immigrants, and particularly Mexicans, Dominicans, and Central Americans, is their low earnings. In addition, per capita household income depends on household size. Thus, for example, despite having higher average incomes compared with blacks, second-generation Mexicans, Puerto Ricans, and Dominicans have slightly lower median per capita incomes because of their larger households. Central Americans fare somewhat better than Mexicans because of both their higher earnings capacity and smaller average households.

Additionally, Hispanics experienced a deterioration in economic well-being over time relative to whites, whose incomes have risen more when times were good and fallen less during recessions.[61] The median household income of Hispanics averaged 74 percent of that of whites during the early

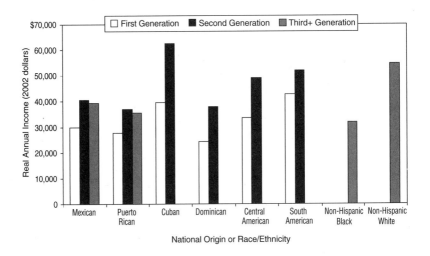

FIGURE 5-4 Median total household income by Hispanic national origin or race/ethnicity and generation.
NOTES: Includes only households whose head is under age 65. Results for Hispanics are shown only for cells with at least 90 observations.
SOURCE: Pooled March CPS files, 1998-2002.

1970s, but eroded following the 1973 oil crisis-induced recession. On the heels of another economic downturn in the early 1980s, the Hispanic-white income ratio deteriorated further, falling below 70 percent in 1985-1988 and again in 1992-1998, reaching its nadir in 1995 at 61 percent.[62] Although white-Hispanic median household incomes converged during the brisk economic growth of the late 1990s, there are signs that the relative income position of Hispanics is eroding yet again.[63] Median incomes of black households were consistently lower than those of Hispanics through-out the period, but over time their income position improved relative to both whites and Hispanics. In 1972, the median black household income was 77 percent that of whites, compared with 90 percent in 2003.[64] Because these comparisons do not separate out native- and foreign-born house-holders, it is difficult to distinguish changes related to increased numbers of low-skill immigrants from those related to business cycle variations. Yet the Survey of Income and Program Participation, one of very few surveys that record annual variation in income, poverty, and wealth, indicates a conver-gence of wealth between native- and foreign-born Hispanics between 1996 and 2001.[65]

Hispanics compensate for low household income through two strategies: income pooling based on extended living arrangements and reli-ance on public benefits (see Figure 5-5). Relative to both whites and blacks, Hispanic households are more likely to include relatives outside the nuclear family, and extended members' average contributions to household income are higher. Extended living arrangements are most common among immi-grant generations but decline thereafter. Mexicans, Central Americans, and Dominicans of the immigrant generation are especially reliant on extended-household members for income pooling, whereas Hispanics with U.S.-born parents largely resemble blacks in their tendency to rely on other relatives for support.

To what extent complex households reflect Hispanic cultural values (familism) versus economic need is unclear. Clearly, however, reliance on this multiple-source income pooling declines over time as the rising prosperity of second and higher generations reduces the need for such compensatory income strategies.

Among Hispanic subgroups, Dominicans and Puerto Ricans under age 65 rely most heavily on public assistance, the second key source of income supplementation. In the case of Puerto Ricans, this largely reflects their high share of single female heads of household; the scarcity of jobs and relatively generous benefit programs in the northeast where many

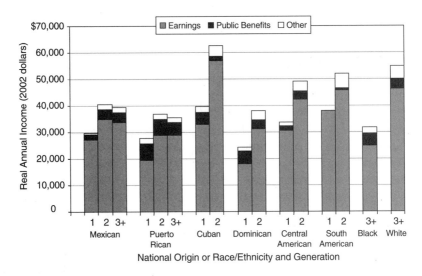

FIGURE 5-5 Sources of median total household income by Hispanic national origin or race/ethnicity and generation.
NOTES: Includes only households whose head is under age 65. Means are simple averages across households, using household weights. Households with zero or negative total income or containing persons with negative income from any source are excluded. Results for Hispanics are shown only for cells with at least 90 observations.
SOURCE: Pooled March CPS files, 1998-2002.

Puerto Ricans live; and the fact that as U.S. citizens, Puerto Ricans (unlike new immigrants) are eligible for public benefit programs. Although second-generation Puerto Ricans rely less than the first generation on income from public benefits, even those born on the mainland depend more on this source of household income compared with other Hispanic subgroups—indeed, at rates more similar to those of blacks. Puerto Ricans' high rates of welfare participation reflect their elevated poverty rates.

Poverty and Wealth Among Hispanics

Trends in median household income conceal the poverty of those at the low end and the prosperity of those at the high end of the income ladder. Indeed, poverty rates dramatize the consequences of poor employment and earnings capacities more effectively than does median household income. Although poverty rates declined during the 1990s—by 3 and 4 percentage points for Hispanics and blacks, respectively—Hispanic poverty held fast at more than 2.5 times the rate among whites.[66] In 1999, more than one in five Hispanics lived below the official poverty line ($16,895 for a family of four or a meager $12 per day per person).[67] Broken out by birthplace, declines in poverty were smallest for Puerto Ricans and greatest for Dominicans, who witnessed the largest drop in absolute poverty during the 1990s.[68] Central American immigrants were less likely to be poor than were Mexicans, Puerto Ricans, and Dominicans of the same generation, but their poverty rates were higher than those of South Americans.[69]

The similar overall poverty rates for first-generation Mexicans, Dominicans, and Puerto Ricans have different sources. As the least-educated group, Mexicans have the lowest overall earning capacity, a liability that persists beyond the second generation. Predominantly recent immigrants with limited skills, Dominicans are, like Puerto Ricans, further handicapped by a high incidence of female-headed households. Having only one potential earner exacerbates the effects of women's low average earnings in depressing household income. Combined, these conditions produce income shortfalls that are only minimally compensated by benefit programs.[70]

Poverty is especially pernicious for children because it is associated with many deleterious outcomes, such as low scholastic achievement, adolescent parenting, substance abuse, and violence.[71] In 1999, more than one in four Hispanics under the age of 18 were poor, compared with nearly one in ten whites. Child poverty rates among Dominicans and Puerto Ricans—35 and 33 percent, respectively—were comparable to those of blacks. Cuban and South American youths experienced the lowest rates of poverty, between 16 and 17 percent. Child poverty rates of Mexicans and Central Americans approached the Hispanic population average—28 and 24 percent, respectively—which is well above the 17 percent overall U.S. poverty rate for those under 18.[72] Elevated Hispanic child poverty rates are particularly disturbing because the relatively young age structure of the population implies large and growing numbers of the youthful poor, and because poverty magnifies the challenges of assimilation and integration for the burgeoning second generation.

Poverty levels are also elevated among elderly Hispanics. The elderly are only a small proportion of the Hispanic population today, but their numbers will grow rapidly in the future. Today's elderly provide a glimpse of how current Hispanic workers are likely to fare at advanced ages, depending on whether the present Social Security and Medicare safety nets remain intact. Overall, about one in five elderly Hispanics was poor in 1999, compared with fewer than one in ten whites and one in four blacks. The poverty risk for Hispanic elderly varies according to national origin, reflecting incomes and types of jobs held at younger ages, as well as length of time in the U.S. labor market. Mirroring child poverty differentials, elderly poverty rates are highest for Puerto Ricans and Dominicans—24 and 29 percent, respectively—and lowest for South Americans, at 16 percent.[73] Poverty rates for other groups are close to the elderly Hispanic population average of 20 percent.

Because Hispanics tend to work for employers that do not offer pensions, elderly Hispanic householders rely more on other sources of income than do either blacks or whites. Moreover, except for Puerto Ricans and Cubans, foreign-born Hispanics rely less on Social Security than do whites and blacks because they are less likely to qualify for the benefits even if they work beyond the required 40 quarters. Until recently, the sectors in which many elderly Hispanics worked, such as agriculture and household service, were not covered by Social Security, which accounts for 42 percent of household income for elderly Central and South American immigrants, but close to 60 percent for blacks and island-born Puerto Ricans.[74]

Elderly immigrants who have not completed the required 10 years in covered jobs to qualify for Social Security benefits or whose benefits are low because of a lifetime of low-wage work often qualify for Supplemental Security Income (SSI), which offers less generous benefits than those provided by Social Security.[75] Elderly foreign-born Hispanics (with the exception of South Americans) derive a larger share of their income from SSI than do blacks, signaling their greater vulnerability to poverty, especially during inflationary periods. By qualifying for Social Security at higher rates, U.S.-born elderly Hispanics mitigate this risk to some extent and face better economic prospects relative to blacks.

Less well documented than trends and disparities in Hispanic poverty are changes at the high end of the income distribution—namely wealth. Net worth is a pertinent indicator of economic well-being because it represents assets that can be tapped in times of financial distress. Recent estimates of Hispanic wealth range from 3 to 9 percent of white median wealth.[76] Home equity constitutes the largest component of Hispanic household wealth, about 50 to 60 percent of net worth during the 1996-2002 period.[77] Less easily converted to cash than other assets in the event of financial crisis, home equity is the source of last resort to offset fluctuations in household income. The reversal of nearly two decades of wage stagnation in the late 1990s also allowed Hispanics to participate in the stock market, albeit to a much lesser extent than whites.[78]

Not only is home equity the largest component of household wealth, but it is also a key marker of middle-class status. Home ownership provides access to myriad social amenities that influence overall well-being, including school quality, neighborhood safety, recreation facilities, and access to health care organizations (see below).[79] Although Hispanic home ownership rates rose from 33 to 44 percent between 1983 and 2001, they have been relatively stagnant since the mid-1990s, even as the rates for white householders have climbed.[80] Consequently, the Hispanic-white ownership ratio, which rose from 48 to 64 percent from the mid-1980s to the mid-1990s, eroded to 60 percent by 2001.[81]

Whether the geographic dispersal of Hispanics from areas with higher to those with lower housing costs will reverse this trend remains unclear. Census data for the largest 100 metro areas indicate that both native- and foreign-born Hispanics participated in rising rates of home ownership during the 1990s owing to favorable interest rates, rising incomes, and the pace of housing construction relative to employment growth.[82] For the foreign born, however, ownership rates increased in the traditional settlement hubs while declining in the new destinations. Because the dispersal of Hispanics to new destinations is a relatively recent phenomenon that involves many recently arrived, low-skill immigrants (see Chapter 4), it is conceivable that their lower average home ownership rates will improve over time as they acculturate in their new locales.[83]

HEALTH STATUS AND ACCESS TO CARE

Like other forms of human capital, health status—both physical and psychological—is an asset that requires investments for improvement and maintenance.[84] In addition to nutritious food, regular exercise, and a toxin-free environment, health status depends on a variety of circumstances—some unique to Hispanics and others shared with populations of similar socioeconomic status, some linked to behavior that compromises or promotes health, and others associated with access to care.

Health Status and Behaviors[85]

Like other indicators of integration, Hispanic health status differs according to subgroup, immigrant generation, English proficiency, and degree of acculturation. Puerto Ricans are less healthy, on average, than other Hispanic subgroups, while Mexicans, Central Americans, and South Americans often compare favorably with whites on several health indicators, despite their low average socioeconomic status. For example, the age-adjusted mortality of Hispanics is lower than that of blacks or whites; the exception is Puerto Ricans, whose mortality rates are higher than those of other Hispanic subgroups (see Figure 5-6). Dubbed the Hispanic "epidemiological paradox" or "immigrant health paradox" by researchers, the lower mortality rates of Hispanics relative to those of whites with more favorable socioeconomic status have puzzled social and health scientists since the 1980s. Precise findings differ, but most studies show that foreign-born Mexicans, Central Americans, and South Americans are most likely to experience this advantage. One factor that contributes to their lower mortality is that healthier people are more likely to migrate than the sickly,

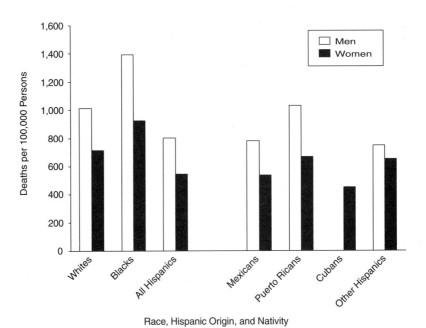

FIGURE 5-6 Age-adjusted mortality for whites, blacks, and Hispanics by sex, 2001.
SOURCE: Arias et al. (2003).

but it is not a sufficient explanation. Why mortality rates are comparable for U.S.-born Hispanics and whites, however, remains a puzzle.

Hispanics also experience favorable birth outcomes in terms of birthweight and infant mortality, another case in which they fare much better than would be expected given their socioeconomic status. In 2001, Hispanics' infant mortality rate of 5.4 per 1,000 live births compared favorably with those of 5.7 for whites and 13.5 for blacks. Cubans (4.2), Central and South Americans (5.0), and Mexicans (5.2) all had lower infant mortality rates than whites, while Puerto Ricans (8.5) fared better than blacks but worse than whites.[86]

Experts often invoke protective cultural and social behaviors of immigrants to explain their advantage in birth outcomes relative to their U.S.-born counterparts. However, since second-generation Hispanic women also have relatively favorable birth outcomes compared with white women of comparable socioeconomic status, cultural explanations do not suffice. Other assets in the Hispanic health ledger include a lower incidence of several major cancers and relatively low rates of activity limitation (e.g., climbing stairs, getting dressed) compared with whites, along with mental health profiles that resemble those of whites. In 2000, for example, the age-adjusted death rate from cancer was 134.9 per 100,000 for Hispanics, compared with 200.6 per 100,000 for whites. Hispanics also smoke less than whites; the exception is Puerto Ricans, who smoke at similar rates.[87]

Hispanics also experience several health liabilities, diabetes and hypertension being by far the most severe. The rising prevalence of Hispanic adults considered overweight or obese likely contributes to higher rates of both conditions, as well as to cardiovascular disease. Although the U.S. epidemic of overweight and obese adults affects all racial and ethnic groups, it is particularly severe for Hispanics. Among Mexicans, 29 percent of men and 40 percent of women are considered obese, compared with 27 percent and 30 percent, respectively, of white men and women.[88]

Trends in overweight among Hispanic youths are particularly worrisome. Hispanic children and adolescents—Mexican and Puerto Rican girls in particular—are much more likely than whites to be overweight. Girls of Mexican origin are nearly twice as likely as white girls to be overweight, while Mexican-origin boys are more than twice as likely as white boys to be overweight. Even more troubling, rates of overweight have risen faster for Hispanic than for white youths (see Figure 5-7). Over the last quarter century or so, the prevalence of overweight preadolescent (ages 6-11) Mexican youths doubled—rising from 13 to 27 percent for boys and from 10 to

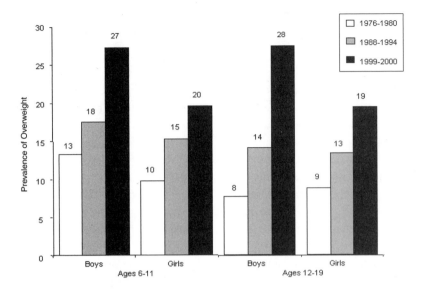

FIGURE 5-7 Time trends in overweight among children and adolescents of Mexican origin, 1976-1980 to 1999-2000.
SOURCE: National Center for Health Statistics (2003) (see Escarce et al., 2006).

20 percent for girls. The rate of adolescents (ages 12-19) considered overweight more than trebled for both boys (from 8 to 28 percent) and doubled for girls (from 9 to 19 percent) over the same period.[89]

Those who claim that acculturation contributes to the rise in Hispanic overweight and obesity point to immigrants' diets, which are richer in fruits and vegetables and lower in fats compared with those of native-born youths, who are more prone to consume high-fat processed and fast foods. Generational differences in diet are mirrored in the prevalence of overweight adolescents, as about one in four first-generation adolescent Hispanics is at risk of being overweight, compared with about one in three second- and third-generation youths.[90]

Several other differences in the health circumstances of Hispanic youths are worth noting. With the exception of Puerto Ricans, Hispanic youths have low rates of asthma, the major chronic disease of childhood. This health asset is offset by their worse oral health compared with their white peers. Hispanic youths also register higher blood lead levels than white children, which places them at greater risk for the adverse effects of lead poisoning on cognitive development.[91]

Hispanic adolescents engage in many health-compromising behaviors, such as use of alcohol and illicit drugs and early sex, at rates comparable to those of white teens, although their tobacco use is lower. Cuban-origin youths have the highest levels of tobacco, alcohol, and drug use, followed by those of Mexican and Puerto Rican origin. By comparison, youths from other Hispanic subgroups have low rates of drug use—probably because larger shares of these subgroups are first-generation immigrants, which means they are less acculturated. In general, acculturated youths engage in such health-compromising behaviors more often than the less acculturated. Hispanic young people also experience poor mental health, exhibiting the highest prevalence of depression of any ethnic group. Although Hispanic adolescent girls are as likely as white adolescents to consider suicide, they are twice as likely to attempt it. Their suicide completion rate, however, is lower than that of other ethnic groups.

The significance of these and other health-compromising behaviors among adolescents transcends their own physical well-being. In 2003, Hispanics had the highest teen birthrate, with 82.2 births per 1,000 adolescent females ages 15-19. In comparison, the birthrate for teens of all backgrounds was 41.7, while that for white teens was 27.5 and for black teens was 64.8.[92] Such statistics bode ill for the educational prospects of Hispanic adolescents, who are more likely than either blacks or whites to withdraw from school if they become mothers.[93] Indeed, all health conditions and behaviors that affect scholastic performance—including not only adolescent childbearing, but also drug and alcohol use and exposure to lead and other environmental contaminants—are especially worrisome because of the lifelong consequences of educational underachievement discussed above.

Access to Quality Care

Hispanics face a variety of financial and nonfinancial obstacles to obtaining appropriate health care. Low rates of insurance coverage are perhaps most notable, but limited access to providers, language barriers, and uneven quality of care exacerbate inequities in health outcomes between Hispanics and whites and between native- and foreign-born Hispanics.

The lack of insurance coverage is greater among foreign-born compared with U.S.-born Hispanics, Spanish compared with English speakers, recent compared with earlier immigrants, and noncitizens compared with citizens. Undocumented immigrants are least likely to be insured; one estimate of their uninsured rates ranges between 68 and 84 percent.[94] Owing to their large shares of recent immigrants, Mexicans and Central and South Americans have the highest uninsured rates. Puerto Ricans and Cubans have the highest insurance rates, with sources of coverage differing between the two groups. Puerto Rican children and working-age adults are much more likely than their Cuban counterparts to obtain health coverage through public insurance programs such as Medicaid and the State Children's Health Insurance Program (SCHIP), but they are less likely to obtain it through an employer (see Figures 5-8a and 5-8b). For Hispanic seniors, eligibility for the Medicare program keeps insurance coverage rates relatively high.

Compared with whites, Hispanics have lower access to employer-provided health insurance because they are more likely than whites to work in small firms, in seasonal occupations, and in part-time jobs.[95] Limited eligibility for public insurance programs, such as Medicaid and SCHIP, further accentuates Hispanics' low coverage rates (with the exception of Puerto Ricans). Many Hispanics—especially Mexicans and Cubans—live in states with restrictive eligibility rules for Medicaid and SCHIP. The federal welfare reforms of 1996 placed further limitations on access to

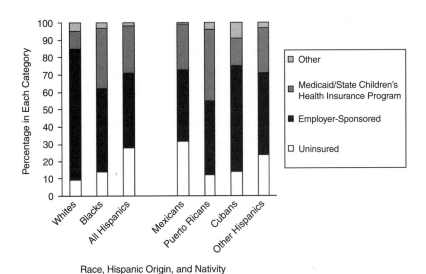

FIGURE 5-8a Health insurance coverage for white, black, and Hispanic children, 1997 to 2001.
SOURCE: 1997 to 2001 Medical Expenditure Panel Survey.

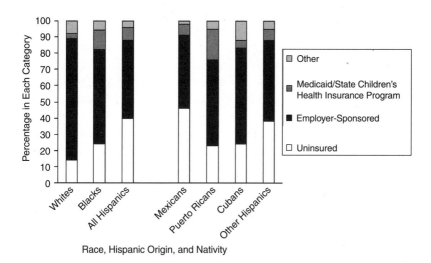

FIGURE 5-8b Health insurance coverage for white, black, and Hispanic working-age adults, 1997 to 2001.
SOURCE: 1997 to 2001 Medical Expenditure Panel Survey.

public health insurance programs for all recent legal immigrants.[96] General confusion about how the new laws affected immigrants triggered declines in their overall utilization of public insurance programs.

Partly because of low rates of health insurance coverage, Hispanics are less likely than whites to have a usual source of care or regular health care provider, which in turn restricts their access to more specialized forms of care. The relatively low number of Hispanic physicians, especially in Hispanics' new destinations, further hinders access to care because Hispanic physicians are more likely than their non-Hispanic counterparts to care for Hispanic patients. Given their large share of recent immigrants, Mexicans are less likely than Puerto Ricans or Cubans to have a usual source of care, as are Spanish speakers compared with English speakers. Furthermore, language barriers undermine quality health care, even among groups with similar demographic and socioeconomic characteristics, by hindering patient-provider communication; by reducing access to health information; and in the worst case, by decreasing the likelihood that sick patients will seek needed care.[97]

Hispanics' low rates of insurance and reduced likelihood of having a regular health care provider mean less preventive care, fewer ambulatory visits, and higher rates of emergency room use compared with whites, although Hispanics' rates of inpatient care are equivalent to those of whites. The preventive services on which Hispanics trail whites include pneumococcal and influenza vaccinations for seniors; mammography, pap smears, and colon cancer screening; blood pressure and cholesterol measurements; and prenatal care for the general population. In 2001, just 75 percent of Mexican and 79 percent of Puerto Rican women received prenatal care in their first trimester, compared with 92 percent of Cuban and 89 percent of white women. Hispanic–white differences in childhood vaccination rates are trivial.[98]

Evidence on the quality of care received by Hispanics is inconclusive, partly because current assessments are based on populations that are not truly representative, such as low-income Medicaid recipients, and partly because results from satisfaction surveys are inconsistent. Nonetheless, Hispanics' reported satisfaction with health care delivery reveals large differences, depending on the degree of English proficiency. In general, Hispanics who speak only Spanish report worse experiences with health care than either whites or Hispanics who speak English. Satisfied patients are more likely to seek care when needed, to comply with provider recommendations, and to remain enrolled in health plans and with specific providers. Paradoxically, and for reasons not fully understood, Spanish-speaking Hispanics rate their physicians and health plans higher than do English-proficient Hispanics, despite admitting to worse care experiences.

To reduce language barriers to health care, the Department of Health and Human Services issued a directive in August 2000 requiring all federally funded programs and providers to offer interpreter services at no cost.[99] Yet only about half of Hispanic patients who need an interpreter receive one. In most cases, the interpreter is a staff person, relative, or friend rather than a trained medical interpreter; in such cases, reported satisfaction rates remain below those of whites.

CONCLUSION

Hispanic integration experiences are as diverse as the eclectic subgroups subsumed under the panethnic identity, but some general trends are discernible. Hispanic families converge in form and function with those of the white majority and rising intermarriage blurs the boundaries of nationality groups. The rise in divorce and nonmarital childbearing over time and across generations signal family decline. The rise of mother-only families bodes ill for economic prospects of the swelling second generation.

There are clear signs of educational progress at all levels both over time and across generations. That other groups also have improved their educational standing has widened attainment gaps, particularly at the college level. Because the fastest-growing and best-paying jobs now require at least some postsecondary education, Hispanics stand to lose economic ground even as their educational attainment rises. Still, employment and earnings trends show clear evidence of economic assimilation, with the greatest gains between the first and second generation. If the most successful third-generation Hispanics "opt out" of Hispanic identity, as available data suggest, economic progress for the third and later generations may well be understated.

Trends in Hispanic home ownership and median household income signal a growing middle class, although the dollar growth of Hispanic household assets is small compared with that recorded by white households.[100] Variation in financial status by immigrant and citizenship status, by age (favoring middle-aged over young householders) and especially by earnings capacity and educational attainment, largely explains the significant gap in economic well-being between Hispanics and whites. As long as this gap persists, however, Hispanics will remain more vulnerable to economic cycles because they have less of a cushion on which to draw during periods of financial distress.

Finally, recent health trends paint the picture of a Hispanic population burdened by the complications of obesity, diabetes, hypertension, and cardiovascular disease, which Americanization appears to worsen rather than improve. The deleterious effects of acculturation are especially evident among second-generation youths and in birth outcomes. Most striking is the high incidence of type 2 diabetes—usually a disease of adults—among young Hispanics and the increased prevalence of multiple risk factors for developing atherosclerosis among children of Mexican origin.[101] These trends foreshadow much higher rates of diabetes and its complications in the future, as large cohorts of Hispanic youths become adults.

The growing number of uninsured Hispanics will place particular stress on the health care safety net—a loosely organized system for delivering care to the uninsured that includes nonprofit organizations, government agencies, and individual providers. By default, some of the responsibility for health care delivery will shift to states and local communities, many of which are already struggling to compensate for shortfalls created by declining federal funding. Experts in both the public and private sectors consider cultural competence—the ability of health systems to provide care to patients with diverse values, beliefs, and behaviors, including tailoring delivery to meet patients' social, cultural, and linguistic needs—to be a crucial component of strategies to reduce disparities in care.[102] Compliance with the federal directive to provide interpreter services at care facilities is especially warranted in new immigrant destinations.

NOTES

1   These findings are documented in greater detail in Landale et al., 2006.

2   Popenoe, 1993.

3   Landale and Oropesa, 2002.

4   Landale and Oropesa, 2002. The evidence for declines in familism among Central and South American nationalities is less clear than is the case for Mexicans because the generational depth is lower.

5   Landale et al., 2006.

6   Lee and Edmonston, 2005.

7   Edmonston et al., 2002, note that all population projections involve higher rates of intermarriage.

8   These findings are documented in greater detail in Schneider et al., 2006.

9   Mare, 1995.

10   See Duncan et al., 2006:Table 6-1.

11   Crosnoe, 2005; Crosnoe et al., 2004; Valencia, 2000.

12   U.S. Department of Education, National Center for Education Statistics, 1999.

13   U.S. Department of Education, National Center for Education Statistics, 1997.

14   U.S. Department of Education, National Center for Education Statistics, 2003b.

15   Carnegie Council on Adolescent Development, 1989.

16   Bryk and Schneider, 2002.

17   U.S. Department of Education, National Center for Education Statistics, 2003b; Valencia, 2002.

18   Bryk and Schneider, 2002.

19   Schneider and Stevenson, 1999.

20   Fry, 2003. This distinction is important because the Hispanic high school dropout rate has been inflated by the presence of foreign-born adolescents who withdrew from school before entering the United States.

21   U.S. Department of Education, National Center for Education Statistics, 2003a: Table 106.

22   Cameron and Heckman, 1993.

23   Fry, 2005; Hirschman, 2001.

24   Carnevale, 1999.

25   Tienda and Simonelli, 2001.

26   Kao and Tienda, 1998.

27   U.S. Department of Education, National Center for Education Statistics, 2002.

28 U.S. Department of Education, National Center for Education Statistics, 2003b.

29 Kim and Schneider, 2004; Portes and Rumbaut, 2001.

30 Fry, 2002, 2003.

31 College Enrollment and Work Activity of Year 2000 High School Graduates. Available: ftp://ftp.bls.gov/pub/news.release/History/hsgec.04132001.news [accessed December 23, 2005].

32 Schneider et al., 2006.

33 Velez, 1985.

34 Alon and Tienda, 2005; Fry, 2004.

35 Clark, 2003; Kochhar, 2004; Wolff, 2004.

36 These findings are documented in greater detail in Duncan et al., 2006.

37 Chiswick, 1978; Schoeni, 1997.

38 The annual employment rate is defined as the percentage of individuals who worked at all during the calendar year preceding the census. Similar results are obtained using annual hours of work as a measure of labor supply.

39 Dominican men also have relatively low employment rates, but nativity differentials for them are small.

40 Duncan et al., 2006:Table 6-4.

41 The estimated deficits are for persons ages 25 to 59 who worked during calendar year 1999, based on regressions by Duncan et al., 2006:Appendix Table A6-7.

42 This is not the case for black men, however, as their 15 percentage point employment deficit would shrink to only 13 percentage points if their human capital endowments were comparable to those of whites.

43 The employment gaps for Puerto Ricans and Dominicans may be due, in part, to their concentration in goods-producing industries in the northeast that have been hurt by deindustrialization, and in part to the fact that their employment patterns are more similar to those of blacks than to those of other Hispanic groups. See DeFreitas, 1991.

44 In contrast to black men, black women's modest earnings disadvantage relative to white women would disappear if they had comparable levels of human capital.

45 Phillips and Massey, 2000; Rivera-Batiz, 1999.

46 See Duncan et al., 2006.

47 Specifically, there is some evidence that darker, more Indian-looking Mexican Americans are vulnerable to discrimination based on skin color. See Allen et al., 2000.

48 Lowell and Fry, 2002.

49 Smith, 2001.

50 Duncan et al., 2006:Table 6-7.

51 Borjas, 1994; Chiswick, 1977; Neidert and Farley, 1985; Perlmann and Waldinger, 1997.

52 Duncan et al., 2006:Figure 5-8.

53 Borjas, 1993; Smith, 2003.

54 Smith, 2003, reports a 4.94-year mean education gap among all first-generation Mexicans (Table 3). This deficit fell to 2.95 years among second-generation Mexicans.

55 Alba and Nee, 1997; Duncan and Trejo, 2005; Telles et al., 2002.

56 Duncan and Trejo, 2005; Duncan et al., 2006; Reimers, 2006.

57 Edmonston et al., 2002; Rutter and Tienda, 2005.

58 Smith, 2003; see Duncan et al., 2006; Reimers, 2006.

59   U.S. Census Bureau; Income 1999. Available: http://www.census.gov/hhes/www/income/income99/99tablea.html [accessed December 27, 2005].

60   Those who were born in the United States have income levels similar to those of whites.

61   U.S. Bureau of the Census, 2004b.

62   U.S. Bureau of the Census, 2004b.

63   Wolff, 2004.

64   The Hispanic-black median income differential exceeded 90 percent between 1995 and 1997, hovering around 94 to 98 percent. See Wolff, 2004:Tables 7 and 8.

65   Kochhar, 2004.

66   Saenz, 2004:Table 11.

67   U.S. Bureau of the Census, 2000c. Poverty thresholds are not adjusted for cost-of-living differences. That large shares of Hispanics live in high-priced cities magnifies the welfare consequences of poverty-level incomes.

68   Saenz, 2004.

69   See Reimers, 2006:Table 7-2.

70   See Reimers, 2006.

71   McLanahan and Sandefur, 1994.

72   U.S. Bureau of the Census, 2000a.

73   U.S. Bureau of the Census, 2000a.

74   Reimers, 2006.

75   Social Security is an "earned" benefit that automatically increases with the cost of living, but SSI is a minimal, means-tested safety net for those elderly who have no other income. Unlike SSI, Social Security is not viewed as "welfare" by the general public. Persons who qualify for Social Security benefits by working most of their adult years in covered jobs, even at a low wage, receive more generous Social Security retirement benefits than persons forced to rely on SSI, the benefit rates of which are below the poverty line.

76   Using the Federal Reserve Board's Survey of Consumer Finances, Wolff, 2004, estimates Hispanic median net worth at 3 percent of the white median for 2001, but Kochhar, 2004, estimates the 2002 median gap at 9 percent—$8,000 versus $89,000—based on the Survey of Income and Program Participation. One source of the difference is that Wolff excludes equity in vehicles and other consumer durables from his estimate of wealth. However, both sets of estimates reveal similar trends, if not levels, for their overlapping period, namely mid-1990s to 2001-2002.

77   Kochhar, 2004:Table 9.

78   Wolff, 2004:26. Stock ownership is concentrated among households in the top quintile of the wealth distribution, accounting for 90 percent of all stock holdings.

79   Clark, 2003.

80   Wolff, 2004.

81   This estimate is close to the .62 for 2000 reported by Fischer and Tienda, 2006, on the basis of census data for the largest 100 metro areas.

82   Fischer and Tienda, 2006; Myers et al., 2005.

83   See Kochhar, 2004.

84   Grossman, 1972.

85 Our emphasis on Mexican-white comparisons reflects the paucity of research comparing other Hispanic nationalities in terms of specific health outcomes. This section draws from Escarce et al., 2006.

86 National Center for Health Statistics, 2003.

87 National Center for Health Statistics, 2003.

88 National Center for Health Statistics, 2003. National data are unavailable on the epidemiology of cardiovascular disease for Hispanics. Moreover, experts disagree about the differences in death rates from heart disease between Hispanics and whites because regional studies have yielded conflicting findings, Escarce et al., 2006.

89 National Center for Health Statistics, 2003.

90 Escarce et al., 2006.

91 Escarce et al., 2006. The Centers for Disease Control and Prevention is currently lowering the threshold blood lead level for intervention from 10 μg/dL to 5 μg/dL. More than one-fourth of preschool-age children and one-fifth of elementary school children of Mexican origin would meet the revised threshold.

92 Ryan et al., 2005.

93 Ahituv and Tienda, 2000.

94 Berk et al., 1999.

95 See Brown and Yu, 2002; Dushi and Honig, 2005; Schur and Feldman, 2001.

96 The 1996 Personal Responsibility and Work Opportunity Reconciliation Act (the federal welfare reform law) barred legal immigrants who entered the United States after August 1996 from receiving federal Medicaid or SCHIP benefits for their first 5 years in the country. Although states can offer coverage for legal immigrants during the 5-year moratorium imposed by the federal regulations, few have elected to do so.

97 Langer, 1999; Ruiz et al., 1992.

98 Escarce and Kapur, 2006. A likely explanation for the shrinking gap in childhood vaccination rates is the Vaccines for Children program, created in 1994, which provides vaccines free of charge to eligible children, including the uninsured.

99 Department of Health and Human Services, 2000.

100 Kochhar, 2004:Tables 17 and 19.

101 Escarce et al., 2006. Other consequences of the overweight epidemic among Hispanic youth include elevated blood pressure and high rates of insulin resistance, hyperinsulinemia, glucose intolerance, and abnormalities in serum lipids. Hispanic youth also have higher triglyceride levels and lower levels of high-density lipoprotein cholesterol than white youth.

102 Betancourt et al., 2002.

Ixrael
Elements (2004)
Copyright by the artist; used with permission of Tropico de Nopal Gallery—Artspace.

6

Uncertain Destinies

As a result of rising immigration from Latin America since 1970 and a swelling second generation, the Hispanic population approached 40 million in 2003, surpassing African Americans as the largest U.S. minority group.[1] Hispanics' high rates of immigration and above-average fertility are projected to continue, making them one of the fastest-growing segments of the U.S. population for the foreseeable future. According to current projections, Hispanics, or people of Hispanic descent, will number about 85 million in 2030—representing almost 1 in 4 U.S. residents.[2]

More than population growth and absolute size, the generational transition now under way will decide the course of Hispanic integration during the 21st century. The proportion of Hispanics who are first-generation immigrants will shrink as demographic growth shifts, once again, from immigration to fertility, accelerating the generational transition. Given the assumptions discussed in Chapter 2, by 2030 just under 1 in 3 Hispanics will be second generation, and a comparable share will be third or higher generation. Although this represents a modest increase since 2000, when just over 1 in 4 Hispanics were second generation, the generational change is profound for two reasons. First, the numbers involved are significant—26 million versus 10 million. Second, the age structure involved is dramatically different (see Figure 6-1).

For the nation, the youthful Hispanic population represents a significant demographic dividend not available to other industrialized countries

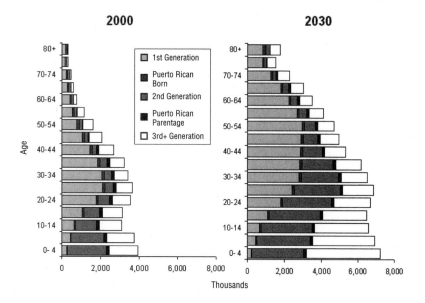

FIGURE 6-1 Hispanic generations by age, 2000 and 2030.
SOURCE: Passel (2004).

that are experiencing population aging (see Chapter 4). This dividend will only be realized, however, if the high school and college graduation gaps between Hispanics and other groups are eliminated or at least significantly narrowed. With a median age of 12.6 in 2000, the majority of the Hispanic second generation is now of school age; by 2030, the majority of the Hispanic second generation will be in the labor force, with a median age of 24.[3] Because most young people have completed their formal schooling by this age, the long-term economic future of Hispanics depends crucially on the educational progress of the second generation, both in absolute terms and relative to other groups they will compete with in the labor, housing, and consumer markets.

Certain aspects of Hispanics' social and economic future can be predicted with some confidence by extrapolating the likely consequences from well-defined trends. Given the considerable uncertainty regarding the future course of immigration and intermarriage, the vitality of the U.S. economy, geopolitical relations with our southern neighbors, and political mobilization initiatives, other conclusions are necessarily tentative. Despite many uncertainties, current trends suggest numerous opportunities, and some risks, for the U.S. Hispanic population and the nation as a whole. The main body of this chapter discusses the main opportunities and risks, extrapolating from recent trends and identifying strategies to deal with likely risks. First, however, we summarize what is known about Hispanic identity, assimilation, and socioeconomic mobility.

DIVERSITY, IDENTITY, AND ASSIMILATION

Hispanicity as a Panethnic Identity

Despite their growing national visibility and regional dispersal, Hispanics are not easily classified racially or ethnically. Moreover, categorization will be even more difficult in the future as intermarriage blurs ethnic, racial, and cultural differences. Since 1970, the Hispanic population has become appreciably more diverse in nationality, social class, legal status, and generation, challenging the cohesion of Hispanicity as a cultural identity. Four mechanisms are particularly important for understanding the construction and persistence of Hispanicity as a panethnic identity: the extent to which Hispanics accept and self-identify using panethnic labels, trends in intermarriage, the extent of Spanish-language use, and the proliferation of panethnic labels through the media and official classification schemes.

Although acceptance of panethnic labels has increased, the majority of Hispanic adults continue to prefer identity labels linked to their country of origin. Over time, however, those country-specific labels give some way to panethnic labels as generational transitions erode homeland traditions. Moreover, while only about one in four second-generation Hispanic youths adopts a panethnic identity, they are much more likely than their parents to accept Hispanic or Latino as a *racial* identity. Thus, both ethnicity and race will likely remain salient markers of Hispanic identity for the foreseeable future.

Depending on how the children of ethnically mixed couples define themselves in ethnic terms and, in particular, whether socially successfully Hispanics are more or less likely to acknowledge their ethnic heritage, intermarriage trends also will affect the future size and social contours of the Hispanic population. Recent intermarriage trends point to a softening of some group boundaries. Because there are few three-generation studies of Hispanics, it is difficult to say whether the most successful individuals and families opt out of Hispanic ethnicity. Although empirical evidence is both spotty and mixed, it appears that beyond the second generation, more successful Hispanics are less likely to self-identify or to be identified by others as Hispanic.[4] This highly tentative inference is consistent with patterns of language shift.

Spanish-language use can reinforce Hispanicity as a panethnic identity in the face of rising intermarriage among Latin American nationalities, but two offsetting forces ultimately will decide what the shift away from the Spanish language portends for the persistence of Hispanicity. First, continued immigration from Latin America will slow the rate of language shift, but how much, in what ways, and for what groups will depend on settlement patterns of the foreign born. Second, the geographic dispersal of Hispanics may accelerate the process of linguistic assimilation, which may also dilute the development of a panethnic identity if accompanied by higher rates of intermarriage with non-Hispanics.

Currently, about 28 million U.S. residents—mainly Hispanic—identify as Spanish speakers. Ironically, both their geographic concentration and their residential dispersal generate anxiety that the United States is becoming a linguistically bifurcated nation. Such anxiety is unfounded because, by all indications, Hispanics are following the linguistic paths of prior immigrants in their increasing reliance on English across generations and over time. The proliferation of Spanish in neighborhoods densely populated by immigrants belies the rapid linguistic assimilation evident between the first and second generation, which is nearly complete by the third. This rapid shift to English indicates fluidity in the boundary between Hispanics and non-Hispanics. As a transitional phase of inevitable language shift, bilingualism is not incompatible with English proficiency, which is a requirement for economic mobility, political integration, and social success.

How best to ensure proficiency in English remains highly controversial because there is no consensus on how best to teach non-English-speaking students across the grade spectrum. Many schools serving large Hispanic student populations have instituted programs in bilingual education or in English as a second language to bridge initial language barriers. While well-implemented programs have been shown to reap significant educational gains, program quality varies greatly across schools and districts. For many students, participation in bilingual education courses not only interferes with English mastery, but at times actually contributes to academic failure.[5]

Finally, two institutions play a role in maintaining and reinforcing Hispanicity as a coherent ethnic identity—the media and government. Media references to "the Hispanic market" and advertising agencies' references to "Hispanic consumers" convey Hispanicity as a monolithic identity, defined through contrast with non-Hispanics. Yet apart from Spanish-language programming and publications for the Spanish-dominant population—mainly recent immigrants—there is no agreement about whether the Hispanic market differs sufficiently from other consumer segments to require specialized expertise.[6] Social reality is more complex than is usually conveyed in advertising and standard business models. Most simply, Hispanics may have nonethnic consumer tastes (and non-Hispanics may be attracted to Hispanic food and culture). The crux of the debate is whether growing numbers justify special marketing strategies for Hispanics, other than Spanish-language messages to reach new arrivals.[7]

Traditional Hispanic advertising agencies focus on the Spanish-language marketplace, but Hispanic-centric agencies approach marketing strategies within a multicultural framework that acknowledges both the population's complexity and the fluidity of its Spanish-language usage. Continued demographic growth coupled with unprecedented geographic dispersal might increase the need for multicultural marketing strategies, at least temporarily, but the long-term demand for Spanish-language outlets will depend on the future course of immigration and the rate of linguistic assimilation across generations.[8] Less debatable is the increased purchasing power of Hispanics as their numbers grow and as greater numbers ascend to the middle class.[9]

Government institutions also encourage a slow shift toward panethnic over national-origin identities through the use of the terms "Hispanic" and "Latino" in their data collection activities. The absence of questions about national origin or options to report national origin as an ethnic identity reduces the salience of a national identity relative to panethnic identities for some Hispanics, particularly those from nations with low representation in the United States, such as Uruguay and Bolivia.

It remains unclear whether Hispanicity is a transitory identity of largely symbolic consequence among the culturally assimilated and socially integrated, or whether it will become an enduring marker of minority group status defined by economic disadvantage and buttressed by cultural differences.[10] The answer surely depends on the reception and assimilation of future arrivals; on the social mobility experienced by the second and subsequent generations; and on the economic opportunities afforded by a globalized economy. On all fronts, there are encouraging signs and abundant opportunities, but also some downside risks.

Sociocultural Transformation

Through their large numbers, through intermarriage and through language assimilation Hispanics are increasingly becoming interwoven into the American sociocultural fabric. Their assimilation is a reciprocal process. Even as new immigrants and established Hispanic residents adapt to American society and institutions, Hispanics are transforming the United States socially and culturally.

One unique role Hispanics play in social transformation involves racial identities. Because large numbers of African, indigenous, and European populations have coexisted in Latin America since the colonial period, social understandings of race in that region differ from the black–white color divide that historically characterized the United States. Although racial differences are an important dimension of Latin American stratification systems, race does not generally create the deep schisms found in mainstream U.S. society. Thus, as growing numbers of Hispanics self-identify in racial terms, especially young people born in the United States, they transform traditional racial classification schemes. Hispanics also may soften racial boundaries by infusing Latin American meanings of race into the black–white racial divide. This latter possibility is highly tentative at this time, however; the dimensions of racial identity will depend in part on Hispanics' continued geographic dispersal to areas historically segregated along racial lines and future patterns of intermarriage.

Settlement patterns that concentrated Mexicans in the southwest, Puerto Ricans in the northeast, and Cubans in south Florida also are being transformed by Hispanics' geographic dispersal in response to employment demand in construction, domestic maintenance and repair services, non-durable manufacturing, and personal and household services. Whether Hispanics' geographic dispersal fosters a greater sense of belonging, results in higher levels of acceptance, and accelerates socioeconomic integration is not clear. Escalating hostility toward Hispanic migrants in new suburban destinations, vigilante activity along the U.S. border, proposed federal legislation to prohibit states from issuing driver's licenses to undocumented immigrants, and the targeted deportation of undocumented Hispanic workers in the name of fighting terrorism challenge the integration prospects of recent Hispanic immigrants. The geographic dispersal of the Hispanic population also challenges health care delivery systems and providers unaccustomed to caring for diverse groups of patients, especially as language barriers undermine providers' ability to deliver culturally competent care to the foreign born.

Over generations, the comingling of different Latin American immigrant populations in multiethnic cities could consolidate panethnic Hispanic identity as a racial category, as now experienced by second-generation youth living in Miami and San Diego. Alternatively, cultural diversity accentuated by the dispersal of recent immigrants could repeat the residential segregation patterns that characterize the traditional gateway cities. Which scenarios play out and where they do so hinges on whether Hispanic immigrants settle among blacks, whites, and Asians in their new destinations and, especially, on whether their geographic dispersal sharpens class divisions and increases social isolation. The relative recentness of the Hispanic scattering precludes long-term forecasting.

Finally, Hispanics take part in social transformation through their political participation and civic engagement. Although references to "the" Hispanic vote are a misconception, average differences in voting behaviors and political attitudes between Hispanics and whites are discernible. For example, because Hispanics express higher levels of trust in government than do whites, they also are more supportive of taxation for collective goods, such as education, public services, and social security. Moreover, differences in these political attitudes across national-origin groups are relatively small.

A distinctive, and discouraging, feature of Hispanics' political behavior is their low participation, evident across a range of electoral, civic, and organizational activities. Particularly noteworthy are their lower rates of voter turnout compared with blacks and whites, even among registered voters. Young age structure, low education, and high poverty levels largely explain the low voting rates and low rates of office holding, but the net result is relatively little political influence, particularly noticeable in areas of high Hispanic concentration. That electoral participation and civic engagement of the foreign born rise with time spent in the United States and also across generations imply that Hispanics will have increased political influence as the second generation comes of age. This outcome, however, rests on making educational investments in the young to socialize them politically and prevent pervasive civic disengagement.

The Costs of Assimilation

At the same time that Americanization facilitates social and economic mobility, it also exacts cultural costs. One cost is the erosion of Hispanics' traditional strong commitment to family life, even at the expense of individual well-being. Familism declines across Hispanic generations, especially among Mexicans and Puerto Ricans, the two groups with the greatest generational depth; other groups will likely follow suit. While new family forms could emerge in which family support remains high, it is more likely that acculturation will weaken familism by fostering the individualism that drives many changes in family behavior. The decline of familism and the shift to nuclear family forms will likely erode the protective functions of extended families and kin networks for future generations. Second and later generations face a higher risk of divorce, and youths reared in single-parent families must contend with the myriad deleterious consequences of parent absence.

Acculturation is also associated with worsening health for Hispanics—as it is for all immigrant groups. This trend poses special risks for the Hispanic population because the phenomenon is experienced most extensively by the swelling second generation. In general, U.S.-born Hispanics report the poorest health and the highest levels of risk behaviors; among those born abroad, negative health outcomes and the propensity to engage in risky behaviors increase with length of residence in the United States.

The worsening health status of Hispanic children and adolescents is of particular concern for three major reasons: their large numbers and rapid growth; their lower insurance coverage levels; and the fact that several health indicators—particularly obesity and the resulting abnormalities of glucose metabolism—point to vulnerabilities that will pose formidable health challenges in the future. If unchecked, these trends portend high rates of premature morbidity and mortality as Hispanic youth, particularly those born in the United States, reach adulthood. Averting those health risks will require strategies that both target obesity among Hispanic youths and attempt to preserve the positive health behaviors of Hispanic immigrants.

Trends in Hispanics' utilization of quality health care services also raise several issues for policy makers, health care providers, and the health care system in general. Continued immigration of Hispanics from Mexico and from Central and South America, coupled with their dispersal to new areas unaccustomed to providing care for diverse populations, will challenge providers responsible for delivering health care to low-income Hispanics, and to recent immigrants in particular. Current trends in employer-sponsored health insurance also signal rising numbers of uninsured Hispanic adults and youths over the next few years. Expansion of federally subsidized programs, such as Medicaid and SCHIP, appears unlikely in an era of unprecedented federal budget deficits, which magnifies the health risks facing Hispanics in the years ahead. Because the carrying capacity of the health care safety net differs across communities and according to local economic conditions, its ability to meet the challenge of providing health care for uninsured Hispanics is highly uncertain.

SOCIOECONOMIC MOBILITY

The importance of education for Hispanics' economic success, social integration, and political participation cannot be overstated. Despite continued temporal and intergenerational gains in educational attainment, Hispanic students lag well behind both whites and blacks in years of school completed, but especially in their representation among the college educated. They face multiple risks in U.S. schools that stem from their delayed acquisition of preschool literacy; their parents' limited familiarity with the U.S. education system; and, for large numbers of second-generation youths, delayed exposure to English. Failure to master English before leaving school represents a formidable risk because English proficiency is absolutely necessary for success in the labor market, and it is vital both for navigating health care systems and for meaningful civic engagement. Closing the gap in Hispanics' education would require placing students in high-quality scholastic programs, reinforced by early intervention initiatives, strong dropout prevention efforts, and strategies that promote college attendance and graduation.

Hispanics' low levels of formal schooling and proficiency in English jeopardize their labor market prospects, as reflected in their employment rates, occupational standing, and earnings. Hispanic workers with less than a high school education are relegated to unstable, low-paying jobs that offer few or no social benefits and usually undesirable working conditions. Low education levels and limited English proficiency also explain most of the earnings deficits between native- and foreign-born Hispanics.

Two key findings consistently emerge with respect to Hispanics' labor market position. First, Hispanics' lower average schooling levels are the major source of their labor market inequalities with other groups. Unlike African Americans, for whom discrimination contributes to racial disparities in earnings, Hispanics reap earnings comparable to whites for each year of education attained. Second, most of the generational progress in Hispanics' earnings occurs between the first and second generations, with less clear-cut outcomes thereafter.[11]

The slow growth in the rate at which Hispanics graduate from college is cause for concern because the best-paying jobs now require a college education. In 1999, nearly 6 of 10 jobs required college-level skills, including many that had not required college training in the past.[12] In 1959, only one in four managers and business professionals (such as insurance and real estate agents) held college degrees; by 1997 more than half did so. In such fast-growing occupations as health services, nearly three in four jobs now require some college education. In 1997 two-thirds of office workers had some college education, and almost one-third had college degrees.[13] These trends bode ill for Hispanics as the college graduation gap widens.

Temporal and intergenerational trends in earnings, household income, and home ownership point to the gradual rise of Hispanics, especially the U.S. born, to the middle class. Still, partly because of the weak economic position of immigrants and partly because of persisting education gaps among the native born, Hispanics as a group are losing economic ground relative to whites. The increased generational gaps in wage growth and annual earnings can be traced to two sources: differences in levels of human capital (e.g., schooling, English-language proficiency, and accumulated work experience) and differences in returns to human capital, that is, how groups are compensated for their education, language skills, and workforce experience.

The coming of age of the second generation should improve Hispanics' overall economic well-being because later generations earn higher incomes. Assuming no deterioration in real income, declines in fertility rates would also raise per capita income while lowering poverty rates. However, trends in divorce and family formation could slow households' economic mobility because female-headed households have much lower incomes than those of married couples. If the growth of mother-only families continues its current path, future improvements in Hispanics' economic well-being would not be predicted. It is too soon to know or forecast the long-term effects of welfare reform on Hispanics—especially on groups that rely most heavily on public benefits, such as Dominicans and Puerto Ricans. It is also too early to tell whether the dispersion of Hispanics from California, Texas, and New York to other parts of the country will enable their children to break the chain of poor schools–poor jobs–poverty. Experiences to date provide a mixed picture at best, but one thing is certain: high-quality education promises the burgeoning second generation the opportunity of narrowing income gaps and providing the nation with a demographic dividend.

What can be stated conclusively, therefore, is that lower levels of schooling, English proficiency, and work experience remain a serious impediment to Hispanics' labor market success and, consequently, their ascent to the middle class. In 2000, for example, the 2-year average educational gap between all Hispanics and whites cost about $100 billion in lost earnings.[14] Given the growth in the Hispanic populations that is projected to occur over the next 30 years, the cost of this education gap could rise to $212 billion in current dollars by 2030, taking into account the generational shift.

Unlike labor market disparities produced by discrimination, educational inequities can often be addressed directly through policy instruments. Closing Hispanics' human capital gaps relative to whites would require early and sustained intervention at all levels of the educational system. The benefits of education are crucial for Hispanic youths, and they are also important for the nation. The temporal coincidence of a large Hispanic second generation and an aging white majority represents an opportunity to attenuate the consequences of the nation's rising burden of old-age dependency. However, this opportunity will be short-lived because continued declines in Latin American fertility will not only alleviate labor pressures south of the border, but also shrink the migrant labor streams on which the U.S. economy has come to depend.[15]

As growing numbers of Hispanics join the labor force and replace white retirees, Hispanic workers should be able to attenuate labor shortages such as those experienced by other Western, industrialized countries. To mitigate the effects of the aging U.S. population on social security funds and Medicare, however, the productivity of young workers must be sufficient to compensate for a shrinking workforce.[16]

AN UNCERTAIN FUTURE

Because of their large numbers, relative youthfulness, and geographic dispersal, Hispanics can be expected to affect American society in profound ways even as they experience considerable transformation as a people. The shape their future will take remains highly uncertain, however. Much depends on whether newcomers from Latin America and long-established Hispanic residents join the ranks of the middle class and experience the social mobility that has characterized European immigrants, whether growing numbers of foreign-born Hispanics become citizens and come to express a political voice, whether the obesity among Hispanic children and adolescents and its attendant health consequences are averted, and whether Hispanics' geographic dispersal accelerates their spatial and social integration. Also uncertain is whether the demographic dividend afforded by the Hispanic age bulge will be realized.

The effects of Hispanics on U.S. schools, health care systems, labor markets, and political organizations are occurring even as their own ethnic contours are being reshaped by immigration, intermarriage, new settlement patterns, language shift, and the adoption of collective panethnic identities, as well as by changing definitions of race and emergent racial identities. Because Hispanics' collective and ethnic-specific experiences differ in notable ways from those of African Americans, and because U.S. economic conditions and opportunity structures today differ greatly from those encountered by European immigrants at the turn of the 20th century, the experiences of those groups are not a reliable indicator of how Hispanics will affect the American future.

The Hispanic future will also be shaped by uncertainty about the long-term competitiveness of the U.S. economy as China and India become major players on the international scene, about changes in geopolitical and economic ties with our southern neighbors, and about possibilities for resolving the status of the 8.5 million Hispanics who live and work without the guarantees of legal status. Until the question of legal status is resolved, the social prospects of undocumented immigrants' U.S.-born children will be limited. Although the Supreme Court ruled that no child can be denied access to public education, irrespective of his or her legal status, this ruling does not apply to higher education, which is becoming ever more critical for labor market success.[17]

During the first quarter of the 21st century, the Hispanic age bulge will offer a unique opportunity to improve the common good by attenuating the social and economic costs of an aging majority population while enhancing national productivity and global competitiveness. Realizing this potential will require educational investments that position future entrants into the labor force to compete for high-paying jobs in a service and information economy. Many other benefits—civic integration, adoption of positive health behaviors, wealth accumulation, and social mobility—will follow, though often at the price of cultural distinctiveness.

The opportunity costs of not closing the Hispanic–white education gap are considerable. The most significant medium-term cost is the relegation of adult Hispanic workers to unstable, low-paying jobs at the lowest rungs of the occupational ladder. A longer-term consequence is the intergenerational perpetuation of disadvantage among Hispanics that would result from limiting the opportunities of future generations—a demographic penalty exemplified by the high incarceration rates among U.S.-born Hispanic youth with less than a high school education compared with their foreign-born counterparts.[18]

Notwithstanding uncertainty about future immigration flows and macroeconomic conditions, what is certain is that the current educational profile of Hispanics will undermine their long-term economic, social, and physical well-being and diminish their prospects for social integration and civic engagement. Given the projected growth of the Hispanic population over the next quarter century, compromising the future economic prospects of Hispanics by underinvesting in their education will likely compromise the nation's future as well.

NOTES

1 U.S. Bureau of the Census, 2003.

2 Passel, 2004.

3 Passel, 2004.

4 Duncan et al., 2006.

5 Schneider et al., 2006.

6 Russell, 2005.

7 Citing a December 2003 Nielson study, *HispanTelligence Market Brief* reports that only 11 percent of the total TV households in the top 16 Hispanic states are Spanish-language dominant, while almost 21 percent of the total TV households in these same states are Hispanic.

8 A recent Pew Hispanic Center report claims that Hispanics' views on many topics are influenced by the language in which they obtain news. See Suro, 2004.

9 Hispanic Business Magazine Staff, 2005.

10 Bean and Tienda, 1987. A distinction is made between symbolic ethnicity and minority status to describe Cubans on the one hand and Mexicans and Puerto Ricans on the other.

11 Levy and Murnane, 2004:42.

12 Carnevale, 1999.

13 Duncan et al., 2006. Calculations by V. Joseph Hotz based on employment, earnings, and school differentials.

14 Longman, 2004, points out that because Mexican fertility rates have dropped so dramatically, the country is now aging five times more rapidly than the United States.

15 Longman, 2004.

16 Plyler v. Doe, 1982, No. 80-1538, 628 F.22 448, and No. 80-1934, affirmed.

17 Rumbaut, 2005.

18 Rumbaut, 2005.

References

Ahituv, A., and Tienda, M. (2000). Employment, motherhood, and school continuation decisions of young white, black, and Hispanic women. *Journal of Labor Economics, 22*(1), 115-158.

Alba, R.D. (2004). *Language assimilation today: Bilingualism persists more than in the past, but English still dominates* (unpublished report). Mumford Center for Comparative Urban and Regional Research. Available: http://mumford.albany.edu/children/reports/language_assimilation/language_assimilation_brief.pdf [accessed March 16, 2005].

Alba, R.D., and Nee, V. (1997). Rethinking assimilation theory for a new era of immigration. *International Migration Review, 31*(Winter), 826-874.

Alba, R.D., Logan, J.R., Lutz, A., and Stults, B.J. (2002). Only English by the third generation? Mother-tongue loss and preservation among the grandchildren of contemporary immigrants. *Demography, 39,* 467-484.

Allen, W., Telles, E., and Hunter, M. (2000). Skin color, income and education: A comparison of African Americans and Mexican Americans. *National Journal of Sociology, 12*(1), 129-180.

Alon, S., and Tienda, M. (2005). Assessing the mismatch hypothesis: Differentials in college graduation rates by institutional selectivity. *Sociology of Education, 78,* 294-315.

Arias, E., Anderson, R.N., Hsiang-Ching, K., Murphy, S.L., and Kochanek, K.D. (2003). *Deaths: Final data for 2001* (vol. 52, no. 3). Hyattsville, MD: National Center for Health Statistics.

Bean, F.D., and Tienda, M. (1987). *The Hispanic population of the United States.* New York: Russell Sage Foundation.

Berk, M.L., Schur, C.L., Chavez, L.R., and Frankel, M. (2000, July-August). Health care use among undocumented Latino immigrants. *Health Affairs, 19*(4), 51-64.

Betancourt, J.R., Green, A.R., and Carrillo, J.E. (2002, October). *Cultural competence in health care: Emerging frameworks and practical approaches.* New York: The Commonwealth Fund. Available: http://www.cmwf.org [accessed May 12, 2004].

Borjas, G.J. (1993, January). The intergenerational mobility of immigrants. *Journal of Labor Economics, 11*(1), 113-135.

Borjas, G.J. (1994, July). Long-run convergence of ethnic skill differentials: The children and grandchildren of the great migration. *Industrial and Labor Relations Review, 47*(4), 553-573.

Borjas, G.J. (2003). The labor demand curve is downward sloping: Reexamining the impact of immigration on the labor market. *Quarterly Journal of Economics, 118*(4), 1335-1374.

Brown, E.R., and Yu, H. (2002). Latinos' access to employment-based health insurance. In M.M. Suárez-Orozco and M.M. Páez (Eds.), *Latinos: Remaking America* (pp. 236-253). Berkeley: University of California Press.

Bryk, A.S., and Schneider, B. (2002). *Trust in schools: A core resource for improvement.* New York: Russell Sage Foundation.

Camarota, S.A. (2004, November). *Economy slowed, but immigration didn't: The foreign-born population, 2000-2004.* Available: http://www.cis.org/articles/2004/back1204.html [accessed November 28, 2004].

Cameron, S.J., and Heckman, J.J. (1993). The nonequivalence of high school equivalents. *Journal of Labor Economics, 11*(1), 1-47.

Capps, R., Fix, M.E., Ost, J., Reardon-Anderson, J., and Passel, J.S. (2005). *The health and well-being of young children of immigrants.* Available: http://www.urban.org/url.cfm?ID= 311139 [accessed April 14, 2005].

Card, D. (2001). Immigrant inflows, native outflows, and the local labor market impacts of higher immigration. *Journal of Labor Economics,19*(1), 22-64.

Carnegie Council on Adolescent Development. (1989). *Turning points: Preparing American youth for the 21st century.* New York: Carnegie Corporation of New York.

Carnevale, A.P. (1999). *Education equals success: Empowering Hispanic youth and adults.* Princeton, NJ: Educational Testing Service for Hispanic Association of Colleges and Universities.

Castillo, J. (2003, July 29). Latino? Hispanic? Chicano? *Austin American-Statesman.* Available: http://nl.newsbank.com/nl-search/we/Archives?p_action=list&p_topdoc=91 [accessed December 2005].

Chiswick, B.R. (1977, February). Sons of immigrants: Are they at an earnings disadvantage? *American Economic Review, 67*(1), 376-380.

Chiswick, B.R. (1978, October). The effect of Americanization on the earnings of foreign-born men. *Journal of Political Economy, 86*(5), 897-921.

Choldin, H.M. (1986). Statistics and politics: The Hispanic issue in the 1980 census. *Demography, 23*(3), 403-418.

Clark, W.A.V. (2003). *Immigrants and the American dream: Remaking the middle class.* New York: Guilford Press.

Crosnoe, R. (2005). Double disadvantage or signs of resilience? The elementary school contexts of children from Mexican immigrant families. *American Educational Research Journal, 42*(2), 269-303.

Crosnoe, R., Kirkpatrick, M., and Elder, G.H., Jr. (2004). School size and the interpersonal side of education: An examination of race/ethnicity and organizational context. *Social Sciences Quarterly, 85*(5), 1259-1274.

Danziger, S. (2004). *Poverty and low-wage work 40 years after the declaration of war on poverty.* Unpublished manuscript, University of Michigan, Ann Arbor.

Danziger, S., and Gottschalk, P. (Eds.). (1995). *Uneven tides: Rising inequality in America.* New York: Russell Sage Foundation.

Davis, K. (2003, June 16). Area's new labor force: Immigrants. *Crain's Chicago Business.*

de la Garza, R.O., DeSipio, L., García, F.C., García, J.A., and Falcón, A. (1992). *Latino voices: Mexican, Puerto Rican, and Cuban perspectives on American politics.* Boulder, CO: Westview Press.

DeFreitas, G. (1991). *Inequality at work: Hispanics in the U.S. labor force.* New York: Oxford University Press.

Department of Health and Human Services. (2000, December). *Assuring cultural competence in health care: Recommendations for national standards and an outcomes-focused research agenda.* (The Office of Minority Health, vol. 65, no. 247, pp. 80865-80879.) Available: http://www.omhrc.gov/clas/cultural1a.htm [accessed April 22, 2005].

DeSipio, L. (2006). Latino civic and political participation. In National Research Council, *Hispanics and the future of America* (Ch. 11). Panel on Hispanics in the United States, Committee on Population, Division of Behavioral and Social Sciences and Education. Washington, DC: The National Academies Press.

DeSipio, L., Pachon, H., de la Garza, R., and Lee, J. (2003). *Immigrant politics at home and abroad: How Latino immigrants engage the politics of their home communities in the United States.* Claremont, CA: Tomás Rivera Policy Institute.

Duncan, B., Hotz, V.J., and Trejo, S.J. (2006). Hispanics in the U.S. labor market. In National Research Council, *Hispanics and the future of America* (Ch. 7). Panel on Hispanics in the United States, Committee on Population, Division of Behavioral and Social Sciences and Education. Washington, DC: The National Academies Press.

Duncan, B., and Trejo, S.J. (2005). *Ethnic identification, intermarriage and unmeasured progress by Mexican Americans.* (Report No. 113423, NBER Working Papers National Bureau of Economic Research, Inc.) Orebro University, Sweden.

Durand, J., Telles, E., and Flashman, J. (2006). The demographic foundations of the Latino population. In National Research Council, *Hispanics and the future of America* (Ch. 3). Panel on Hispanics in the United States, Committee on Population, Division of Behavioral and Social Sciences and Education. Washington, DC: The National Academies Press.

Dushi, I., and Honig, M. (2005, March). *Offers or take-up: Explaining minorities' lower health insurance coverage.* Available: http://www.umich.edu/~eriu/conferences/vpops_papers.html [accessed April 2005].

Edmonston, B., Lee, S.M., and Passel, J.S. (2002). Recent trends in intermarriage and immigration and their effects on the future racial composition of the U.S. population. In J. Perlmann and M.C. Waters (Eds.), *The new race question: How the Census counts multiracial individuals* (pp. 227-255). New York: Russell Sage Foundation.

Edmonston, B., and Passel, J.S. (Eds.) (1994). *Immigration and ethnicity: The integration of America's newest arrivals.* Washington, DC: Urban Institute Press.

Escarce, J.J., and Kapur, K. (2006). Access to and quality of health care. In National Research Council, *Hispanics and the future of America* (Ch. 10). Panel on Hispanics in the United States, Committee on Population, Division of Behavioral and Social Sciences and Education. Washington, DC: The National Academies Press.

Escarce, J.J., Morales, L.S., and Rumbaut, R.G. (2006). The health status and health behaviors of Hispanics. In National Research Council, *Hispanics and the future of America* (Ch. 9). Panel on Hispanics in the United States, Committee on Population, Division of Behavioral and Social Sciences and Education. Washington, DC: The National Academies Press.

Fears, D. (2003). Latinos or Hispanics? A debate about identity. *The Washington Post*, August 25. Available: http://web.posc.jmu.edu/methods/readings/latino%20vs%20hispanic% 20labels.pdf [accessed July 2005].

Fehr, H., Jokisch, S., and Kotlikoff, L.J. (2004, November). *Fertility, mortality, and the developed world's demographic transition* (CESifo Working Paper No. 1326). Presented at CESifo summer workshop, Venice, Italy.

Fischer, M.J., and Tienda, M. (2006). Redrawing spatial color lines: Hispanic metropolitan dispersal, segregation, and economic opportunity. In National Research Council, *Hispanics and the future of America* (Ch. 4). Panel on Hispanics in the United States, Committee on Population, Division of Behavioral and Social Sciences and Education. Washington, DC: The National Academies Press.

Fix, M., and Zimmermann, W. (2001, June). *All under one roof: Mixed status families in an era of reform.* Available: http://www.urban.org/url.cfm?ID=409100 [accessed July 14, 2004].

Freeman, R.B. (1993). How much has deunionization contributed to the rise in male earnings inequality. In P. Gottschalk and S. Danziger (Eds.), *Uneven tides; rising inequality in America* (pp. 133-163). New York: Russell Sage Foundation.

Fry, R. (2002). *Latinos in higher education: Many enroll, too few graduate.* Washington, DC: Pew Hispanic Center.

Fry, R. (2003). *Hispanic youth dropping out of U.S. schools: Measuring the challenge.* Washington, DC: Pew Hispanic Center.

Fry, R. (2005). *The higher dropout rate of foreign-born teens: The role of schooling abroad.* Washington, DC: Pew Hispanic Center.

Ginsburg, R., and Moberg, D. (2004, September). *The economic contribution of non-native (immigrant) Hispanics to Nevada.* Reno: Progressive Leadership Alliance of Nevada, Center on Work and Community Development.

Grossman, M. (1972). On the concept of health capital and the demand for health. *Journal of Political Economy, 80,* 223-255.

Haney López, I. (2004). *Race on the 2010 Census: Hispanics and the shrinking white majority.* Center for the Study of Law and Society Jurisprudence and Social Policy Program. Paper presented at the Center for the Study of Law and Society bag lunch speaker series, October 6, paper 18. Available: http://repositories.cdlib.org/csls/lss/18 [accessed August 25, 2005].

The Henry J. Kaiser Family Foundation. (2000). *National survey of Latinos in America.* (The Washington Post/Kaiser Family Foundation/Harvard University Survey Project.) Menlo Park, CA: Author.

Hirschman, C. (2001). The educational enrollment of immigrant youth: A text of the segmented-assimilation hypothesis. *Demography, 38,* 317-336.

Hispanic Business Inc. (2005). *HispanTelligence market brief. Latest research: U.S. Hispanic media markets, 2000-2007.* Santa Barbara, CA: Author. Available: http://www.hispanicbusiness.com/news/newsbyid.asp?id=19490 [accessed January 2006].

Hispanic Business Magazine Staff. (2005). Hispanintelligence Report. *Hispanic Business Magazine,* January/February issue.

Immigration and Naturalization Service. (2003). *Estimates of the unauthorized immigrant population residing in the United States: 1990 to 2000.* Available: http://uscis.gov/graphics/shared/aboutus/statistics/2000ExecSumm.pdf [accessed June 24, 2005].

International Communications Research. (2004, June 15). *Hispanic identity in the United States: A focus group summary report.* Media, PA: Author.

Jasso, G., and Rosenzweig, M.R. (1990). *The new chosen people: Immigrants in the United States.* New York: Russell Sage Foundation for the National Committee for Research on the 1980 Census.

Kandel, W., and Cromartie, J. (2004). *New patterns of Hispanic settlement in rural America.* (U.S. Department of Agriculture, Economic Research Service.) Available: http://www.ers.usda.gov/publications/rdrr99 [accessed March 18, 2005].

Kao, G., and Tienda, M. (1998). Educational aspirations of minority youth. *American Journal of Education, 106,* 349-384.

Kim, D., and Schneider, B. (2004). *Social capital in action: Alignment of parental support in adolescents' transition to postsecondary education.* Unpublished paper, presented at American Sociological Association Annual Meeting, August 16.

Kochhar, R. (2004, October). *The wealth of Hispanic households: 1996 to 2002.* Washington, DC: Pew Hispanic Center.

Kochhar, R., Suro, R., and Tafoya, S. (2005, July). *The new Latino south: The context and consequences of rapid population growth.* Washington, DC: Pew Hispanic Center.

Kuck, C.H. (2005). *Immigration today: Who made this mess?* Presentation to the Century Foundation Board of Directors. White Bear Lake, MN.

Landale, N.S., and Oropesa, R.S. (2002). White, black, or Puerto Rican? Racial self-identification among mainland and island Puerto Ricans. *Social Forces, 81,* 231-254.

Landale, N.S., Oropesa, R.S., and Bradatan, C. (2006). Hispanic families in the United States: Family structure and process in an era of family change. In National Research Council, *Hispanics and the future of America* (Ch. 5). Panel on Hispanics in the United States, Committee on Population, Division of Behavioral and Social Sciences and Education. Washington, DC: The National Academies Press.

Langer, N. (1999). Culturally competent professional in therapeutic alliances enhance patient compliance. *Journal of Health Care for the Poor and Underserved, 10*(1), 19-26.

Lee, J., and Bean, F.D. (2004). America's changing color lines: Immigration, race/ethnicity, and multiracial identification. *Annual Review of Sociology, 30,* 221-242.

Lee, S.M., and Edmonston, B. (2005). *New marriages, new families: U.S. racial and Hispanic intermarriage.* (Population Bulletin, 60, No. 2.) Washington, DC: The Population Reference Bureau.

Levy, F. (1995). Incomes and income inequality. In R. Farley (Ed.), *State of the union: America in the 1990s* (vol. 1, Economic Trends). New York: Russell Sage Foundation.

Levy, F. (1998). *The new dollars and dreams: American incomes and economic change.* New York: Russell Sage Foundation.

Levy, F., and Murnane, R.J. (2004). *The new division of labor: How computers are creating the next job market.* Princeton, NJ: Princeton University Press.

Logan, J.R. (2003). *American newcomers.* Albany, NY: Lewis Mumford Center, State University of New York.

Logan, J.R., Stults, B., and Farley, R. (2004). Segregation of minorities. In P. Longman, The global baby bust. *Foreign Affairs* (vol. 83, no. 3). Washington, DC: Council on Foreign Relations.

Longman, P. (2004). *The empty cradle: How falling birthrates threaten world prosperity and what to do about it.* New York: Basic Books.

Looff and Associates. (1999, December). *Distribution of low wage workers by firm size in the U.S.* Final report prepared for the U.S. Small Businesses Administration, Office of Advocacy. Available: http://smealsearch2.psu.edu/11113.html [accessed September 23, 2004].

López, D.E. (1978). Chicano language loyalty in an urban setting. *Sociology and Social Research, 62,* 267-278.

López, D.E. (1996). Language: Diversity and assimilation. In R. Waldinger and M. Bozorgmehr (Eds.), *Ethnic Los Angeles* (pp. 139-159). New York: Russell Sage Foundation.

Lowell, L.B., and Fry, R. (2002, March). *Estimating the distribution of undocumented workers in the urban labor force: Technical memorandum to how many undocumented (The numbers behind the U.S.-Mexican migration talks).* Washington, DC: Pew Hispanic Center.

Mare, R. (1995). Changes in educational attainment and school enrollment. In R. Farley (Ed.), *State of the union: America in the 1990s* (pp. 155-214). New York: Russell Sage Foundation.

Massey, D.S., Durand, J., and Malone, N.J. (2002). *Beyond smoke and mirrors: Mexican immigration in and era of economic integration.* New York: Russell Sage Foundation.

McLanahan, S., and Sandefur, G. (1994). *Growing up with a single parent: What hurts, what helps?* Cambridge, MA: Harvard University Press.

Montejano, D. (1987). *Anglos and Mexicans in the making of Texas, 1836-1986.* Austin: University of Texas Press.

Myers, D., Pitkin, J., and Park, J. (2002). Estimation of housing needs amidst population growth and change. *Housing Policy Debate, 13*(3), 567-596.

Myers, D., Pitkin, J., and Park, J. (2005). *California demographic futures: Projections to 2030, by immigrant generations, nativity, and time of arrival in U.S.* Los Angeles: University of Southern California, School of Policy, Planning, and Development.

National Center for Health Statistics. (2003). *Health, United States, 2003.* (DHHS Publication No. 2003-1232.) Hyattsville, MD: Author.

National Council of La Raza. (2004). *State of Hispanic America 2004: Latino perspectives on the American agenda.* Washington, DC: National Council of La Raza.

Neidert, L.J., and Farley, R. (1985). Assimilation in the United States: An analysis of ethnic and generation differences in status and achievement. *American Sociological Review, 50*(6), 840-850.

Olson, J., and Jordon, S. (2003). On the job of last resort: Meat plant risks extend to nightly cleanup work. Special Report. *Omaha World-Herald,* Sunrise Edition, October 12.

Orfield, G., Losen, D.J., Wald, J., and Swanson, C. (2004). *Losing our future: How minority youth are being left behind by the graduation rate crisis.* (Harvard University: The Civil

Rights Project.) Available: http://www.civilrightsproject.harvard.edu/research/dropouts/dropouts_gen.php [accessed June 25, 2005].

Passel, J.S. (2004). *Methodology and assumptions for population estimates and projections by race and generation, 1960 to 2030.* (Paper prepared for Panel on Hispanics in the United States.) Unpublished paper, Pew Hispanic Center, Washington, DC.

Passel, J.S. (2005, March). *Estimates of the size and characteristics of the undocumented population.* Washington, DC: Pew Hispanics Center.

Perlmann, J., and Waldinger, R. (1997). Second generation decline? Children of immigrants, past and present: A reconsideration. *International Migration Review, 31*(4), 893-922.

Pew Hispanic Center. (2004, October 18). *Wealth gap widens between whites and Hispanics.* (Wealth report.) Washington, DC: Author.

Pew Hispanic Center, Assimilation and Language. (2004, March). *Survey brief.* Washington, DC: Author.

Pew Hispanic Center/Kaiser Family Foundation. (2002). *2002 National survey of Latinos.* Available: http://pewhispanic.org/reports/report.php?ReportID=15 [accessed December 3, 2002].

Phillips, J.A., and Massey, D.S. (2000). Engines of immigration: Stocks of human and social capital in Mexico. *Social Science Quarterly, 81,* 33-48.

Plyler v. Doe. (1982). No. 80-1538, 628 F.22 448, and No. 80-1934, affirmed.

Popenoe, D. (1993). American family decline, 1960-1990: A review and appraisal. *Journal of Marriage and Family, 55,* 527-555.

Porter, E. (2005). Illegal immigrants are bolstering social security with billions. *The New York Times,* Section A (Business/Financial Desk), April 5, p. 1.

Portes, A., and Rumbaut, R.G. (2001). *Legacies: The story of the immigrant second generation.* Berkeley and New York: University of California Press and Russell Sage Foundation.

Reimers, C. (2006). Economic well-being. In National Research Council, *Hispanics and the future of America* (Ch. 8). Panel on Hispanics in the United States, Committee on Population, Division of Behavioral and Social Sciences and Education. Washington, DC: The National Academies Press.

Rivera-Batiz, F.L. (1999). Undocumented workers in the labor market: An analysis of the earnings of legal and illegal Mexican immigrants in the United States. *Journal of Population Economics, 12*(1), 91-116.

Ruiz, M.S., Marks, G., and Richardson, J.L. (1992). Language acculturation and screening practices of elderly Hispanic women: The role of exposure to health-related information from the media. *Journal of Aging and Health, 4*(2), 268-281.

Rumbaut, R.G. (2004). Ages, life stages, and generational cohorts: Decomposing the immigrant first and second generations in the United States. *International Migration Review, 28*(3), 1160-1205.

Rumbaut, R.G. (2005). Turning points in the transition to adulthood: Determinants of educational attainment, incarceration, and early childbearing among children of immigrants. *Ethnic and Racial Studies, 28*(6), 1041-1086.

Rumbaut, R.G. (2006). The making of a people. In National Research Council, *Hispanics and the future of America* (Ch. 2). Panel on Hispanics in the United States, Committee on Population, Division of Behavioral and Social Sciences and Education. Washington, DC: The National Academies Press.

Russell, J. (2005, April). Shop shifting: Hispanic advertising agencies face an identity crisis between integration and specialization. *Hispanic Business,* 18-20.

Ryan, S., Franzetta, K., and Manlove, J. (2005, February). *Hispanic teen pregnancy and birth rates: Looking behind the numbers* (Research Brief). Washington, DC: Child Trends.

Sachs, S. (2001). The world: What's in a name? Redefining minority. *The New York Times,* Section 4 (Week in Review), March 11, p. 1.

Saenz, R. (2004). *Latinos and the changing face of America.* New York: Russell Sage Foundation and Population Reference Bureau.

Schneider, B., and Stevenson, D. (1999). *The ambitious generation: America's teenagers, motivated but directionless.* New Haven, CT: Yale University Press.

Schneider, B., Martinez, S., and Owens, A. (2006). Barriers to educational opportunities for Hispanics in the United States. In National Research Council, *Hispanics and the future of America* (Ch. 6). Panel on Hispanics in the United States, Committee on Population, Division of Behavioral and Social Sciences and Education. Washington, DC: The National Academies Press.

Schur, C.L., and Feldman, J. (2001, May). *Running in place: How job characteristics, immigrant status, and family structure keep Hispanics uninsured.* Available: http://www.cmwf.org/publications/publications_show.htm?doc_id=221348 [accessed March 2, 2005].

Smith, J.P. (2001). Race and ethnicity in the labor market: Trends over the short and long term. In N.J. Smelser, W.J. Wilson, and F. Mitchell (Eds.), *America becoming: Racial trends and their consequences* (vol. II, pp. 52-97). Washington, DC: National Academy Press.

Smith, J.P. (2003). Assimilation across the Latino generations. *American Economic Review,* *93*(2), 315-319.

Stavans, I. (2003). *Spanglish.* New York: Harper Collins.

Suro, R. (2004, April). *Changing channels and crisscrossing cultures.* Available: http://pewhispanic.org/reports.print.php?ReportID=27 [accessed May 11, 2005].

Suro, R. and Passel, J.S. (2003, October*). The rise of the second generation: Changing patterns in Hispanic population growth.* Washington, DC: Pew Hispanic Center.

Suro, R., Fry, R., and Passel, J.S. (2005, June). *Hispanics and the 2004 election: Population, electorate and voters.* Washington, DC: Pew Hispanic Center.

Tafoya, S. (2004, December). *Shades of belonging: Latinos and racial identity.* Washington, DC: Pew Hispanic Center.

Telles, E. (2004). *Race in another America.* Princeton, NJ: Princeton University Press.

Tienda, M. (2002). Demography and the social contract. *Demography, 39*(4), 587-616.

Tienda, M., and Simonelli, S. (2001). Unplugging the pipeline: Hispanics in higher education and affirmative action. In Institute of Medicine, *The right thing to do, the smart thing to do: Enhancing diversity in health professions. Summary of the Symposium on Diversity in Health Professions in Honor of Herbert W. Nickens, M.D.* (pp. 117-142). B.D. Smedley, A.Y. Stith, L. Colburn, and C.H. Evans (Eds.). Nickens Symposium Advisory Committee. Washington, DC: National Academy Press.

Tyson, L.D. (2004). How Bush widened the wealth gap: Not since the '20s has income inequality been this great. *Business Week,* September 27.

U.S. Bureau of the Census. (2000a). *We the people: Hispanics in the United States.* (Special Report CENSR-18). Washington, DC: Author, Ethnic and Hispanic Statistics Branch, Population Division.

U.S. Bureau of the Census. (2000b). IPUMS. In S. Ruggles, M. Sobek, T. Alexander, C.A. Fitch, R. Goeken, P.K. Hall, M. King, and C. Ronnander (Eds.), *Integrated Public Use Microdata Series: Version 3.0* [Machine-readable database]. Minneapolis, MN: Minnesota Population Center.

U.S. Bureau of the Census. (2000c). *Poverty 1999: Poverty thresholds in 1999.* Available: http://www.Census.gov/hhes/poverty/threshld/thresh99.html [accessed January 26, 2005].

U.S. Bureau of the Census. (2003, June 18). *Young, diverse, urban: Hispanic population reaches all-time high of 38.8 million.* Washington, DC: Author. Available: http://www.Census.gov/ Press-Release/www/releases/archives/hispanic_origin_population/00 [accessed July 5, 2004].

U.S. Bureau of the Census. (2004a). *Census Bureau news.* Washington, DC: Author. Available: http://www.census.gov/press-release/www/releases/archives/race/001839.html [accessed June 14, 2004].

U.S. Bureau of the Census. (2004b). *Historical income tables: Households, Table 5.* Available: http://www.Census.gov/hhes/income/histinc/h05.html [accessed March 11, 2004].

U.S. Bureau of the Census. (2005). *Hispanic population passes 40 million.* Available: http:// www.census.gov/Press-Release/www/releases/archives/population/005164.html [accessed August 18, 2005].

U.S. Department of Education, National Center for Education Statistics. (1997). *America's teachers: Profile of a profession, 1993-94.* (NCES 97-460, R.R. Henke, S.P. Choy, X. Chen, S. Geis, and M.N. Alt, eds.) Washington, DC: Author.

U.S. Department of Education, National Center for Education Statistics. (1999). *National household education survey.* (Parent Interview Component, public-use data, weighted.) Washington, DC: Author.

U.S. Department of Education, National Center for Education Statistics. (2002). *The condition of education.* (Based on 1998 High School Transcripts Study.) Washington, DC: Author.

U.S. Department of Education, National Center for Education Statistics. (2003a). *Digest of education statistics, 2002.* (NCES 2003-060, T.D. Snyder and C.M. Hoffman, eds.) Washington, DC: U.S. Author.

U.S. Department of Education, National Center for Education Statistics. (2003b). *Status and trends in the education of Hispanics.* (NCES 2003-008.) Washington, DC: Author.

U.S. Department of Homeland Security. (2003). *Undocumented emigration to the United States, 1951 to 2003* (apprehensions). Washington, DC: Office of Immigration Statistics, Yearbook of Immigration Statistics.

Valencia, R.R. (2000). Inequalities and the schooling of minority students in Texas: Historical and contemporary conditions. *Hispanic Journal of Behavioral Sciences, 22*(4): 445-459.

Valencia, R.R. (2002). *Chicano school failure and success: Past, present, and future.* New York: Routledge/Falmer Press.

Velez, W. (1985). Finishing college: The effects of college type. *Sociology of Education, 58*(3), 191-200.

Verba, S., Schlozman, K.L., and Brady, H.E. (1995). *Voice and equality: Civic voluntarism in American politics.* Cambridge, MA: Harvard University Press.

Watson Wyatt Worldwide. (2004*). International pension readiness report finds most industrial countries unprepared for coming crisis.* Available: http://www.watsonwayatt.com/news/featured/wef [accessed November 5, 2004].

Weber, J., Symonds, W.C., and Lee, L. (2004, September). Health insurance: Small biz is in a bind. *Business Week.* Available: http://www.businessweek.com/@@*712hYcQWTJfTxoA/magazine/content/04_39/b3901047_mz011.htm [accessed October 9, 2004].

Wolff, E.N. (2004, May). *Changes in household wealth in the 1980s and 1990s in the U.S.* (Working Paper No. 407.) New York: The Levy Economics Institute of Bard College.

Appendix A

Methods

POPULATION PROJECTIONS

An analysis commissioned from Dr. Jeffrey Passel of the Pew Hispanic Center provided data on population growth for the period 1960-2000 for the Hispanic population and other racial/ethnic groups; alternative scenarios for the same period using the multigeneration projection methodology developed by Edmonston and Passel[1]; and multigeneration projections for 2000-2030, again for Hispanics and all others. This analysis produced data on the historical contributions made by immigration and high fertility levels to the growth of the Hispanic population. It also yielded projections of likely future levels of Hispanic immigration and fertility and an idea of how the United States would look if national borders had been sealed after 1960. A detailed discussion of the analysis methodology and results is provided in Passel (2004).[2]

FOCUS GROUPS

To explore views on Hispanic identity among Hispanics living in different parts of the United States and of varying generational status, the National Academies, in conjunction with the Pew Hispanic Center, commissioned International Communications Research to conduct focus group interviews with adult Hispanics. Five broad themes were discussed: labels and terminology for identity, components of identity, language, inter-personal relationships, and sense of belonging/societal relations.

Altogether, 10 focus groups were convened in five cities between February 10 and May 17, 2004, with 98 first-, second-, and third-generation Hispanics ages 18 to 31.[3] The locations were chosen to sample residents of areas with established concentrations of Hispanics (e.g., Los Angeles), as well as residents of new areas where Hispanic communities are emerging (e.g., Raleigh). Eight of the groups were conducted in English and two in Spanish.

The focus group participants were randomly selected from Hispanic households in the five cities using community-based recruiting. To enhance the size of the sample frame as well as the representativeness of the focus group participants, the sampling combined several standard recruitment approaches, including intercepts; referrals; recruiter databases; and responses to ads posted in community centers, churches, and shopping areas frequented by the Hispanic population in each city.

CENSUS ADJUSTMENTS

This report uses adjusted figures from the 2000 census to estimate the size of the Hispanic population. By reallocating individuals classified as "other Hispanic" in published tabulations, this adjustment produces a more accurate tally of the size of specific groups. It does not affect the total count of Hispanics in the United States. The 2000 census reported about 5 million people who checked "other Spanish, Hispanic, or Latino" but did not indicate a specific ethnicity or national origin. However, about 2 million of them in fact reported a specific Spanish-speaking Latin American country of birth or ancestry in response to the questions on the long form. This additional information was used to assign these persons to a specific national-origin group. For all Hispanic groups, the adjusted figures are shown in Table A-1.

CURRENT POPULATION SURVEY

The Current Population Survey (CPS) is an important primary data source for intergenerational analysis. Since 1980, the decennial censuses have been constrained by the deletion of the parental nativity question that was asked from 1870 to 1970, making it impossible to distinguish the first and second (foreign-parentage) generations from each other and from third

TABLE A-1 Original and Adjusted Census Estimates, 2000

Group	Original Figures (%)	Adjusted Figures (%)
Mexican	58	63
Puerto Rican	10	10
Cuban	4	4
Other Hispanic or Latino	28	8
Salvadoran, Guatemalan		4
Dominican		3
Central American, other		3
Colombian		2
Peruvian, Ecuadorian		2
South American, other		1
Hispanic Total	100	100

SOURCES: U.S. Bureau of the Census (2000b, Summary File 1), Rumbaut (2006).

and later generations. Since 1994, however, the annual CPS has included items on maternal and paternal country of birth, permitting inter-generational analysis. Authors of several chapters of *Hispanics and the Future of America*, the companion to this report, used a common file of the March CPS for the years 1998, 1999, 2000, 2001, and 2002, including specially constructed variables for Hispanic ethnicities (defined by subjective self-identification and country of birth) and generational cohorts defined by age at arrival and nativity of self and parents.

EXPERT TESTIMONY

To obtain expert testimony on selected topics, the panel held several workshops. The topics and invited presenters were as follows.

- Defining and Measuring the Hispanic Population
  Jorge Del Pinal, U.S. Bureau of the Census
  Elizabeth Martin, U.S. Bureau of the Census
  Jeffrey Passel, Urban Institute

- Residential Segregation
  John Iceland, University of Maryland

- Crime and Criminal Justice
  Bruce Western, Princeton University
  Jeff Morenoff, University of Michigan
  Patricia Fernández-Kelly, Princeton University

- Education Transitions and Hispanic Students
  Sean Reardon, Pennsylvania State University
  Claudia Galindo, Pennsylvania State University
  Catherine Riegle-Crumb, University of Texas at Austin
  Chandra Muller, University of Texas at Austin
  Eugene Garcia, Dean, College of Education, Arizona State University
  Maria Lopez-Freeman, Executive Director, California Science Project
  Roberto Gonzalez, Principal, Sam Houston High School
  Jerry Valadez, K–12 Science Coordinator, Fresno Unified School District

- Hispanic Adolescents' Health
  Marilyn Winkleby, Stanford University
  William Vega, Robert Wood Johnson Medical School

- Media and Marketing
  John Gallegos, Gallegos Group
  J. Gerardo Lopez, La Opinión

NOTES

1 Edmonston and Passel, 1994.
2 Passel, 2004.
3 For more information, refer to International Communications Research, 2004.

Appendix B

Biographical Sketches
of Panel Members and Staff

MARTA TIENDA (*Chair*) is Maurice P. During '22 professor in demographic studies and professor of sociology and public affairs at Princeton University and former director of the Office of Population Research. She has held appointments at the University of Chicago, where she served as chair of sociology, and the University of Wisconsin. She is a fellow of the American Academy of Arts and Sciences, the American Academy of Political and Social Sciences, and the American Association for the Advancement of Science, as well as past president of the Population Association of America. She serves as board member of the Federal Reserve Bank of New York, the Princeton Medical Center, the Sloan Foundation, the Jacobs Foundation of Switzerland, and the Corporation of Brown University. Her coauthored and coedited publications include *The Hispanic Population of the United States* (1987), *Divided Opportunities* (1988), *The Color of Opportunity* (2001), *Youth in Cities* (2002), and *Ethnicity and Causal Mechanisms* (2005). She has a Ph.D. in sociology from the University of Texas at Austin.

LOUIS DeSIPIO is an associate professor in the Department of Political Science and the Chicano/Latino Studies Program at the University of California, Irvine (UCI). His research focuses on Latino politics, the process of political incorporation of new and formerly excluded populations into U.S. politics, and public policies such as immigration, immigrant settlement, naturalization, and voting rights. He is the author of *Counting on the Latino*

Vote: Latinos as a New Electorate (1996) and the coauthor of *Making Americans/Remaking America: Immigration and Immigrant Policy* (1998). He is also the author and editor of a seven-volume series on Latino political values, attitudes, and behaviors. He served as interim director of the University of Illinois at Urbana-Champaign Latina/Latino Studies Program from 1999 to 2002 and the acting director of the UCI Chicano/Latino Studies Program in 2004. He serves as graduate director in the UCI Department of Political Science and undergraduate advisor in the Chicano/Latino Studies Program.

JORGE DURAND is professor of anthropology at the University of Guadalajara, México, and codirector of the Mexican Migration Project and the Latin American Migration Project sponsored by Princeton University and the University of Guadalajara. He is a member of the Mexican Academy of Sciences and a foreign associate of the National Academy of Sciences. He has studied and written about Mexican migration to the United States for the past 20 years. His publications in this field include *Return to Aztlán* (1987), *Más allá de la línea* (1984), *Miracles on the Border* (1995), *Migrations Mexicaines aux Etats-Unis* (1995), *La experiencia migrante* (2000), *Beyond Smoke and Mirrors* (2002), and *Clandestinos: Migración mexicana en los albores del siglo XXI* (2003).

JOSÉ J. ESCARCE is professor of medicine at the David Geffen School of Medicine at the University of California, Los Angeles, and senior natural scientist at the RAND Corporation. His research interests include racial and ethnic disparities in health and health care, immigrant health, provider and patient behavior under economic incentives, technological change in medicine, and the impact of health care market structure on costs and quality. He has served on the National Advisory Council for Health Care Policy, Research, and Evaluation of the U.S. Department of Health and Human Services; was a member of the Institute of Medicine's Committee on Understanding and Eliminating Racial and Ethnic Disparities in Health Care; and is senior associate editor of the journal *Health Services Research*. He serves on the board of education of the public school district in Santa Monica, California, a small urban district where one-third of the students are Hispanic. He is a graduate of Princeton University and has an M.S. in physics from Harvard University and M.D. and Ph.D. degrees, the latter in health economics, from the University of Pennsylvania.

V. JOSEPH HOTZ is professor of economics at the University of California, Los Angeles (UCLA), and research associate at the California Center for Population Research and the National Bureau of Economic Research. He also serves as chair of the oversight board of the California Census Research Data Center and received a fellow award from the Econometric Society. Previously he was chair of the Department of Economics at UCLA and a member of the social science and population peer review panel of the National Institutes of Health. His research interests include labor economics, economic demography, and applied economics. He is currently coprincipal investigator on numerous projects, including ones on tax policy and low-wage labor markets and designing new models for explaining family change and variation. He has written and published many articles on such topics as family change, teenage childbearing, and income tax. He has M.S. and Ph.D. degrees in economics from the University of Wisconsin-Madison.

NANCY S. LANDALE is professor of sociology and demography at the Pennsylvania State University. Her research focuses on family patterns and health outcomes of racial and ethnic minorities in the United States, especially Hispanic populations. She has written extensively about the roles of migration and assimilation in the family patterns and infant health outcomes of Puerto Ricans. She was the principal investigator for the Puerto Rican Maternal and Infant Health Study, a study of infant health among mainland and island Puerto Ricans. Articles from the study have focused on the role of selective migration in infant mortality; the role of assimilation in health behaviors and stress; the financial and nonfinancial contributions of nonresident, cohabiting, and married fathers; and the influence of skin color on low birthweight. She was a member of the National Research Council's Committee on the Health and Adjustment of Immigrant Families and Children.

FAITH MITCHELL is a senior program officer at the National Academies, where she has been on the staff since 1995. Her professional experience includes ethnographic field research, academic appointments, philanthropy, and government service. She is coeditor of several National Research Council reports, including *Terrorism: Perspectives from the Behavioral and Social Sciences*; *Discouraging Terrorism: Some Implications of 9/11*; *America Becoming: Racial Trends and Their Consequences*; *Governance and Opportu-*

nity in Metropolitan America; and *Premature Death in the New Independent States.* Her doctorate is in medical anthropology.

CORDELIA REIMERS is professor emerita of economics at Hunter College and the Graduate School of the City University of New York (CUNY), where she taught from 1982 to 2003. In recent years she has also been a senior economist at the Council of Economic Advisers in Washington and a visiting scholar at the Russell Sage Foundation. Prior to joining the faculty of CUNY, she was an assistant professor of economics and public affairs at Princeton University. Her research has focused on racial and ethnic differences in labor market outcomes and on Social Security and retirement behavior. Recent papers concern the effects of welfare reform on low-skilled New Yorkers and the effects of 9/11 on low-skilled minority and immigrant workers in New York City. She has a B.S. in history from the University of Wisconsin-Madison and a Ph.D. in economics from Columbia University.

RUBÉN G. RUMBAUT is professor of sociology at the University of California, Irvine, and co-director of its Center for Research on Immigration, Population and Public Policy. He is the founding chair of the section on international migration of the American Sociological Association and a member of the National Research Council's Committee on Population. He codirects the Children of Immigrants Longitudinal Study, begun in 1991 as well as a new large-scale study of Immigration and Intergenerational Mobility in Metropolitan Los Angeles. He coauthored *Immigrant America: A Portrait; Origins and Destinies: Immigration, Race and Ethnicity in America; California's Immigrant Children: Theory, Research, and Implications for Educational Policy; Immigration Research for a New Century: Multidisciplinary Perspectives;* and *On the Frontier of Adulthood: Theory, Research, and Public Policy.* The book he coauthored with Alejandro Portes, *Legacies: The Story of the Immigrant Second Generation,* won the distinguished scholarship award of the American Sociological Association and the W.I. Thomas and Florian Znaniecki award for best book in the immigration field. A native of Havana, Cuba, he has a Ph.D. in sociology from Brandeis University.

BARBARA SCHNEIDER is professor of sociology and human development at the University of Chicago and will join the faculty at Michigan State University as the John A. Hannah chair in the School of Education in fall 2005. She currently directs the Data Research and Development Center, and codirects the Alfred P. Sloan Center on Parents, Children, and Work. Interested in the lives of adolescents and their families and schools, she has written widely on these topics. She is the coauthor of *The Ambitious Generation: America's Teenagers, Motivated But Directionless*; *Becoming Adult: How Teenagers Prepare for the World of Work*; and *Trust in Schools: A Core Resource for Improvement*. She and Linda Waite have recently completed a book based on findings from the Sloan 500 Family Study exploring the lives of working families. She is currently conducting a new random assignment project, TEACH Research, designed to improve adolescents' transition to college. She serves on a number of advisory boards including the American Educational Research Association grants board. Recently, she was selected by the American Sociological Association as the new editor of *Sociology of Education*.

EDWARD TELLES is professor of sociology at the University of California, Los Angeles. He has published widely in the area of immigration, race and ethnic relations, social demography, and urban sociology. In 2004-2005, as a visiting scholar at the Russell Sage Foundation, he wrote a large part of a book on intergenerational change among Mexican Americans, based on random sample surveys of Los Angeles and San Antonio in 1965 and 2000. He was program officer in human rights for the Ford Foundation in Rio de Janeiro from 1997 to 2000. He has received awards from the National Institute of Child and Human Development, the National Science Foundation, and the Fulbright Commission. He will be the 2006 recipient of the distinguished scholarly publication award from the American Sociological Association for his book *Race in Another America: The Significance of Skin Color in Brazil*. In 2005, he received the Otis Dudley Duncan award from the population section from the same association. He has a B.A. in anthropology from Stanford University and a Ph.D. in sociology from the University of Texas at Austin.

STEPHEN TREJO is an associate professor of economics at the University of Texas at Austin. Previously he was a member of the economics faculty at the University of California, Santa Barbara. His research focuses on public policy issues involving labor markets, including overtime pay regulation, the experiences of immigrants, and obstacles to the economic progress of minority groups. He has a Ph.D. in economics from the University of Chicago.

Appendix C

Contents
Hispanics and the Future of America

1 Introduction: *E Pluribus Plures* or *E Pluribus Unum?*
  Marta Tienda and Faith Mitchell

2 The Making of a People
  Rubén G. Rumbaut

3 The Demographic Foundations of the Latino Population
  Jorge Durand, Edward Telles, and Jennifer Flashman

4 Redrawing Spatial Color Lines: Hispanic Metropolitan Dispersal,
  Segregation, and Economic Opportunity
  Mary J. Fischer and Marta Tienda

5 Hispanic Families in the United States: Family Structure and
  Process in an Era of Family Change
  Nancy S. Landale, R. Salvador Oropesa, and Cristina Bradatan

6 Barriers to Educational Opportunities for Hispanics in the
  United States
  Barbara Schneider, Sylvia Martinez, and Ann Owens

7   Hispanics in the U.S. Labor Market
     Brian Duncan, V. Joseph Hotz, and Stephen J. Trejo

8   Economic Well-Being
     Cordelia Reimers

9   The Health Status and Health Behaviors of Hispanics
     José J. Escarce, Leo S. Morales, and Rubén G. Rumbaut

10 Access to and Quality of Health Care
     José J. Escarce and Kanika Kapur

11 Latino Civic and Political Participation
     Louis DeSipio

Index

A

Access to health care, 103–106
  future prospects, 107–108, 122–123
  insurance costs and, 58
  language barriers, 105, 106
  prenatal care, 106
  preventive services, 106
  quality of care, 106
  U.S.-born children of undocumented
    immigrants, 32
  U.S. social services policy, 58
Adolescents
  childbearing patterns, 25, 103
  obesity trends, 101–102, 111 n101
  substance use, 102
Advertising and marketing, 118–119,
  127 n7
Age at immigration, language
  proficiency and, 48
Age structure of Hispanic population, 3,
  23
  childbearing patterns, 25
  future prospects, 7, 14, 60–64, 115–
    116, 125, 126

  poverty patterns, 97–98
  socioeconomic implications, 61–64,
    125, 126
Agriculture, 27–29, 66
Aid to Families with Dependent
  Children, 58
Alcohol use, 103
American Community Survey, 51, 53
  n31
Amnesty programs, 30–31
Arizona, 64
Assimilation
  distinguishing features of Hispanic
    experience, 5–6, 57
  ethnic/racial identity, 45
  health status and, 102, 107, 122
  language use, 46, 118
  process, 4–5, 37
  tradition of familism and, 78, 121–
    122
  trends among Hispanic population,
    5
  See also Social integration
Asthma, 102
Atherosclerosis, 8, 102

B

Birth rate among immigrant
populations, 6, 23–24
Bolivians, 27
Border control, 30, 31–32
Bracero Accords, 27–29
Brazil, 20

C

California, 21, 64, 65–66
Cancer, 101
Cardiovascular disease, 8, 111 *n*88
Census practices
concept of race, 40–45
ethnic categories, 4, 21, 37, 38–40,
50, 51, 52 *n*8
parental birthplace questions, 50, 51
strategies for improving, 50, 51
use of surname as ethnic identifier,
39, 52 *n*7
Childbearing patterns
among youth, 25, 103
economic outcomes and, 124
educational attainment and, 24, 25
Hispanic family characteristics, 24
immigrant *vs.* native-born, 25
nonmarital, 24–25, 78, 79, 106–107
prenatal care, 106
Civil Rights movement (1960s), 38
Clinton administration, 58
Cohabitation, 79, 80
College enrollment and graduation, 7
economic outcomes and, 59, 124
expectations and aspirations, 85, 86
obstacles to, 86–87
trends, 87, 123, 124
tuition assistance, 58
two-year colleges, 87
Colombians, 44, 65
Construction industry, 66, 67
Country of origin
diversity within Hispanic population,
19–20, 23, 38

educational attainment patterns, 82
employment rate variation, 88
ethnic self-identification and, 37,
117
geographic distribution in U.S., 21–
22
household income and, 94
language proficiency and, 46
political orientation and, 69
poverty patterns, 97
undocumented immigrants, 27
U.S. population growth, 26–27
wage rates and, 90
See also specific immigrant group
Criminal justice, 16 *n*2
Cubans, 70
access to health care, 104
attitudes toward government, 70
childbearing patterns, 79
educational attainment, 82
employment rate, 88
ethnic/racial identity, 41, 44
family characteristics, 24, 78
geographic distribution of immigrant
population, 21–22
household income, 94
immigration patterns, 22
infant mortality, 101
intergenerational earnings patterns,
92
language proficiency of immigrants
from, 46
poverty patterns, 97
prenatal care, 106
Current Population Survey, 51

D

Depression, 103
Diabetes, 8, 101, 107
Diet and nutrition, 102
Directive 15 (OMB), 38–39, 41, 45
Discrimination
against dark-skinned Mexicans, 109
*n*47

early U.S. history, 21
  teacher bias, 84
Diversity within Hispanic population,
  19, 32, 38
  economic well-being, 87–88
  ethnic identity and, 4, 50, 117
  family structure and functioning, 78
  political orientation, 68–69
  recent patterns, 26–27
Divorce trends, 78–79
Dominicans, 65
  educational attainment, 24
  employment patterns, 90
  employment rate, 109 *n*43
  ethnic/racial identity, 41, 44
  family structure and functioning, 78
  household income, 94
  immigration patterns, 27
  language preferences and proficiency,
    49
  poverty patterns, 97, 98
  welfare participation, 95

E

Economic status
  age patterns, 97–98
  distribution patterns, 58–59
  diversity within Hispanic population,
    87–88
  educational attainment and, 8–9,
    107, 123, 124–125
  family structure and, 8, 94, 95, 124
  future prospects, 99, 116
  generational change, 91–93
  home ownership, 68, 98, 99, 107
  household income, 93–96
  motivation of undocumented
    immigrants, 27
  obstacles to advancement, 124–125
  poverty rates, 96–98
  trends, 5, 107, 124
  wealthy Hispanics, 98–99
  See also Employment; Wages
Ecuadorians, 44, 65

Educational attainment
  and childbearing patterns, 24, 25
  college enrollment and graduation,
    7, 14, 59, 86–87, 124
  consequences of underinvestment in
    young Hispanic population, 3–4,
    8–9, 14, 15–16, 126–127
  cultural value, 86
  employment and economic
    outcomes, 5–6, 8–9, 14, 59, 60,
    61, 89–90, 93, 107, 123–124,
    125
  foreign-born *vs.* U.S. born Hispanics,
    5, 46, 81–82
  future challenges, 3–4, 14, 64, 68,
    116, 123, 124, 126–127
  General Equivalency Diploma, 86
  guidance counseling and, 85, 86
  health factors, 103
  high school performance/graduation,
    7, 14, 85–86
  language proficiency and, 48, 123
  mathematics instruction, 86–87
  middle school performance, 84–85
  patterns and trends, 7, 14, 46, 80–
    82, 107, 123–124
  political participation and, 71
  preschool home environment and,
    82–84, 123
  primary school performance, 84
  strategies for improving, 123, 125
  See also School system
Employment
  access to health care and, 58, 104
  educational attainment and, 8, 14,
    60, 89–90, 93, 123–124
  future challenges, 14, 59–60, 125
  immigrant *vs.* second generation, 5–
    6, 67
  implications of aging patterns, 61–64
  job market trends, 6, 59, 66–67
  language proficiency and, 8, 46, 89–
    90
  Mexican presence in U.S., 20, 21
  patterns and trends, 3, 6, 7, 14, 66–
    67, 88–91

public perception of low-wage
    Hispanic workers, 32
See also Undocumented workers;
    Wages
Ethnic identity. *See* Identity

F

Family structure and functioning
    assimilation effects, 78, 121–122
    diversity within Hispanic population,
        78
    economic status and, 8, 94, 95, 124
    familism in, 77–78, 122
    future prospects, 78, 79–80, 106–
        107, 122
    income pooling, 95
    intermarriage effects, 79, 80
    preschool literacy, 82–84
    size of families, 24, 79
    Spanish language use at home, 46, 48
    trends, 8, 78–79
    U.S.-born children of undocumented
        immigrants, 32
    See also Childbearing patterns
Filipino immigrants, 39
Florida, 22, 64, 65, 66
Future prospects, 15–16, 125–127
    age profile of U.S. population, 14,
        61–64
    consequences of underinvestment in
        young Hispanic population, 3–4,
        8–9, 14, 15–16
    cost of education gap, 8–9, 14
    demographic patterns, 6, 7, 13, 115
    determinants of Hispanic experience,
        57, 125–126
    economic status, 99, 116, 125
    family structure and functioning, 8,
        78, 79–80, 106–107, 122
    health care access and delivery, 8,
        107–108, 120, 122–123
    home ownership, 68
    intermarriage outcomes, 80
    language preferences and proficiency,
        49–50

meaning of Hispanic identity, 37,
    38, 45, 117–119
political effectiveness, 72, 73, 121
predictability, 116–117
race relations, 6, 45, 120
residential segregation, 67–68
sources of Hispanic population
    growth, 6, 25, 115
strategies for increasing English
    proficiency, 7–8, 118
welfare reform and, 8, 124

G

Generational differences
    attitudes toward language, 48–49
    earnings, 90–93, 124
    ethnic/racial identity, 44–45
    language preference and proficiency,
        47–48
    See also Immigrants; Second
        generation Hispanics; Third and
        later generations
Geographic distribution
    by country of origin, 21–22
    home ownership patterns, 68, 99
    implications for health care, 122
    implications for social integration,
        67–68, 120–121
    residential segregation patterns, 65–
        66, 67–68
    roots of Hispanic culture in
        Americas, 20–21
    trends, 3, 6, 19, 57, 64–65, 120
    undocumented immigrants, 31
Georgia, 64
Guatemalans, 27, 44
Guyana, 20

H

Haitians, 44
Hart-Celler Act. *See* Immigration and
    Nationality Act (1965)
Head Start, 84

Health care
    future challenges, 8, 120, 122–123
    Hispanic physicians, 105
    primary care providers, 105–106
    U.S. social services policy, 58
    See also Access to health care; Health
        status; Insurance, health
Health status, 15
    birth outcomes, 101
    determinants of, 99–100
    mortality, 100–101
    patterns and trends, 8, 100–103,
        107, 122
    See also Access to health care; Health
        care
Hispanics, defined, 4
Hispanics and the Future of America, 14–
    15
Historical context
    Cuban presence in U.S., 22
    Hispanic immigration, 15
    immigration law and policy, 27–32
    Mexican presence in U.S., 21–22
    Puerto Rican presence in mainland
        U.S., 22
    race relations in Latin America, 41,
        52 *n*10, 120
    racial and ethnic identity categories,
        38–40, 52 *n*1
    roots of Hispanic culture in
        Americas, 20–22
Home ownership
    home equity value, 98, 99
    trends, 68, 99, 107
Household income, 5, 93–96, 107
Hypertension, 101

I

Identity, 15
    assimilation process, 4–5, 37
    census categories, 4, 21, 37, 38–44,
        50, 51, 52 *n*7–8
    diversity within Hispanic
        populations and, 4, 50, 117

economic assimilation and self-
        identification, 92–93
    future prospects, 37, 38, 45, 50,
        117–119
    intermarriage issues, 80, 117–118
    language and, 38, 118
    media advertising and marketing,
        118–119
    national origin and, 37, 117
    racial identification, 4, 40–45, 50,
        117
    terminology, 4, 16 *n*2, 20, 37, 40,
        52 *n*1–3
Illegal Immigration Reform and
        Immigrant Responsibility Act
        (1996), 30, 31
Immigration/Immigrants
    access to health care, 103–104, 122–
        123
    childbearing patterns, 25
    demographic trends, 6, 19, 23–24,
        25–27, 61
    distinguishing features of Hispanic
        experience, 5–6, 15, 23, 32, 45–
        46, 57
    earnings patterns, 90–91
    educational attainment patterns, 7,
        81–82
    employment patterns, 67, 88
    geographic distribution in U.S., 21–
        22
    Hispanic population growth without,
        25–26
    language preference and proficiency
        patterns, 46, 47–48
    political participation patterns, 71
    U.S. policy, 57–58
    See also Undocumented immigrants;
        specific immigrant group
Immigration and Nationality Act (1965)
        (Hart-Celler Act), 29
Immigration Reform and Control Act
        (1986), 30–31
Infant mortality/morbidity, 101
Insurance, health
    future challenges, 8, 122–123

patterns and trends, 58, 103–106
U.S.-born children of undocumented
immigrants, 32
Inter-Agency Committee on Mexican
American Affairs, 39
Intermarriage
assimilation process, 5
familism and, 79, 80
identity issues, 13, 80, 117–118
International comparisons, population
size, 20
Ixrael, 113

J

Jamaicans, 44

L

Language
assimilation process, 5, 7, 118
barriers to health care, 105, 106
characteristics of fluent speakers, 48
distinguishing element of Hispanic
immigrant experience, 45–46
diversity within Hispanic population,
19
employment outcomes, 8, 46, 89–
90, 123
ethnic self-identification and, 38, 118
generational attitudes, 48–49
immigrant patterns, 46, 47–48
non-Spanish speaking Latin
Americans, 20
preschool literacy, 82–83, 123
residential segregation and, 66
significance of, 46, 123
Spanglish, 49
Spanish language use at home, 46,
48
strategies for increasing English
proficiency, 7–8, 118
trends among Hispanic population,
5, 46, 48, 49–50, 118
Latino, defined, 4, 16 *n2,* 37

Law, immigration
demand for immigrant workers and,
27, 31–32
effectiveness, 30–32
historical and conceptual evolution,
27–32
Lomas Garza, Carmen, 1

M

Media advertising and marketing, 118–
119, 127 *n7*
Medicaid, 8, 104, 122–123
Mental health, 103
Mexicans
access to health care, 104
census classification, 21, 39–40
childbearing patterns, 24, 25, 79
educational performance and
attainment, 82
employment trends and patterns,
66–67, 88, 90–92
ethnic/racial identity, 44
family characteristics, 24, 78–79,
122
geographic distribution, 21–22, 64,
65
health status, 100
household income, 94
infant mortality, 101
language proficiency, 46, 48, 49–50
obesity risk, 101–102
poverty patterns, 97
prenatal care, 106
size of U.S. population, 20, 21, 23
undocumented, 27–30
Mexican War, 21
Military, 16 *n2*
Mortality, 100–101

N

Native Americans, 15
Naturalization, immigration law and
rate of, 31

Nevada, 64, 66–67
New Jersey, 64, 66
New Mexico, 21, 64
New York, 64–65
Nicaraguans, 27, 44
North Carolina, 64

O

Obesity, 8, 101–102, 111 n101, 122
Office of Management and Budget, 38–39, 41, 45

P

Panamanians, 65
Paraguayans, 65
Pell grants, 58
Personal Responsibility and Work
    Opportunity Reconciliation Act
    (1996), 58, 111 n96
Peruvians, 27, 44
Political participation, 121
    civic engagement, 70, 121
    diversity of Hispanic interests, 68–69
    educational issues, 69–70
    Hispanic politicians, 71
    strategies for increasing Hispanic
        effectiveness, 71–72, 73, 121
    trust in government, 70, 121
    voting patterns and trends, 70–71,
        121
Political refugees
    from Central America, 26–27
    from Cuba, 22
Population patterns and trends, 3, 7, 13,
    19, 115
    birth rate among immigrant
        populations, 6, 23–24, 25, 115
    countries of origin, 19–20, 23, 26–
        27
    Cuban presence in U.S., 22
    immigration, 6, 19, 23–24, 25–27,
        61

international comparisons, 20
    Mexican presence in U.S., 20, 21–22
    Puerto Rican presence in mainland
        U.S., 22
    size of U.S. Hispanic population, 3,
        6, 13, 19, 20, 22–23, 33 n1, 115
    undocumented aliens, 27, 31, 33
        n14
    without immigration, 25–26
    See also Age structure of Hispanic
        population; Geographic
        distribution
Poverty rates, 96–98
Public Law *94-311,* 38
Public perception and understanding
    of low-wage Hispanic workers, 32
    teacher bias, 84
    trust in government, 70
Public services, access to, 31, 32
    health insurance, 104–105, 122–123
    Social Security, 98
    U.S. policy, 57–58
    See also Access to health care; School
        system; Welfare
Puerto Ricans, 21
    access to health care, 104
    census classification, 39
    childbearing patterns, 24, 25, 79
    educational attainment, 82
    employment rate, 88, 90, 109 n43
    English language proficiency, 46
    ethnic/racial identity, 44
    family characteristics, 24, 78–79,
        122
    geographic distribution of immigrant
        population, 21–22, 64–65
    health status, 100
    household income, 94
    infant mortality, 101
    intergenerational earnings patterns,
        92
    population patterns and trends, 22
    poverty patterns, 97, 98
    prenatal care, 106
    welfare participation, 95–96

R

Race relations
  future prospects, 6, 45
  in Latin America, 41, 52 *n*10, 120
  segregation patterns, 65–66
Racial identity, 40–45, 50, 117. *See also*
    Identity
Religion, 16 *n2*
Rodriguez, Freddy, 75

S

Salvadorans, 27, 44
Sanchez, Juan, cover
School system, 15
  ethnic distribution, 84, 87
  Hispanic educators, 84
  Hispanic political orientation, 69–70
  teacher bias, 84
  U.S. social services policy, 58
  See also Educational attainment
Second generation Hispanics
  birth outcomes, 101
  childbearing patterns, 25
  economic status, 91–93, 94, 124
  educational attainment patterns, 81–
    82
  ethnic/racial identity, 38, 44–45
  future challenges, 116
  health status, 122
  intermarriage among, 80
  language proficiency, 46, 47
  political participation patterns, 71
  population patterns and trends, 3, 6,
    23, 25, 60–61, 115
  social impact, 3, 60–61
September 11 terrorist attacks, 32
Service industries, 66–67
Smoking, 101
Social impact of Hispanic population
    trends
  age profile of U.S. population and,
    14, 60–61, 115–116, 125, 126

  consequences of underinvestment in
    young Hispanic population, 3–4,
    8–9, 14, 15–16, 125, 126–127
  future prospects, 3–4, 6, 13, 115–
    117, 125–127
  political participation and, 121
  race relations, 6, 120
Social integration
  future challenges, 3–4, 6, 14, 121
  geographic distribution of Hispanic
    population and, 67–68, 120–121
  Hispanic identity and, 50
  intermarriage and, 80
  language proficiency and, 7, 46
  political participation, 68–72
  public perceptions as obstacles to, 32
  residential segregation and, 65–66,
    67–68
  U.S.-born children of undocumented
    immigrants, 32
  See also Assimilation; Race relations
Social Security participation, 98, 110
    *n*75
Spain, 20–22
Spanglish, 49
Spanish-American War, 21
State Children's Health Insurance
    Program, 8, 104, 122–123
Stock market investment, 98–99
Substance use, 103
Suicidal behavior/ideation, 103
Supplemental Security Income, 98, 110
    *n*75
Surinam, 20

T

Tax policy, 70
Temporary Assistance to Needy
    Families, 58
Terminology of ethnic identity, 4, 16
    n2, 20, 37, 40, 52 *n*1–3, 119
  concept of race, 40–45
Texas, 21, 64

Third and later generations
demographic trends, 115
earnings patterns, 91–93
ethnic self-identification, 92–93,
107, 117–118
language preference and proficiency,
47–48, 49
Treaty of Guadalupe-Hidalgo, 21
Tufiño, Nitza, 35

U

Undocumented immigrants
access to health care, 103–104
access to public services, 31
amnesty programs, 30–31
countries of origin, 27
economic and political context, 27,
31–32
employment. *See* Undocumented
workers
estimated number, 27, 31, 33 *n*14
immigration law and policy, 27–32,
126
method of entry, 31
naturalization patterns, 31
policy challenges, 32–33, 126
recent patterns, 30
social stresses for, 32
U.S.-born children of, 32
Undocumented workers
estimated number, 5
law and policy, 27–29, 31–32
sanctions on employers of, 30, 31–
32
See also Undocumented immigrants

Urban population
educational experiences, 85
home ownership, 99
labor market trends, 67
segregation patterns, 65–66, 67–68
trends, 3, 6, 64–65

V

Vaccination, 106, 111 *n*98
Valdez, Julio, 11
Valdez, Patssi, 55
Vargas, Kathy, 17

W

Wages
distribution patterns, 58–59
educational attainment and, 8–9, 14,
59, 90
generational change, 90–93
immigrant experience, 5
influences of immigrant labor, 59
minimum wage, 59
national origin and, 90
patterns and trends, 5, 59, 90
See also Economic status;
Employment; Household income
Welfare
future prospects, 8, 124
trends, 95–96
U.S. policy, 58
Women
childbearing patterns. *See*
Childbearing patterns
employment patterns and trends, 88,
90